JOH
TR
T

THE LABOUR PARTY
SINCE 1945

WITHDRAWN

A

A

LIVERPOOL JMU LIBRARY

3 1111 00662 0130

British History in Perspective

General Editor: Jeremy Black

PUBLISHED TITLES

C. J. Bartlett *British Foreign Policy in the Twentieth Century*
Jeremy Black *Robert Walpole and the Nature of Politics
in Early Eighteenth-Century Britain*
D. G. Boyce *The Irish Question and British Politics, 1868–1968*
Keith Brown *Kingdom or Province? Scotland and the Regal Union, 1603–1715*
John W. Derry *British Politics in the Age of Fox, Pitt and Liverpool*
Ann Hughes *The Causes of the English Civil War*
Ronald Hutton *The British Republic, 1649–1660*
Kevin Jefferys *The Labour Party since 1945*
D. M. Loades *The Mid-Tudor Crisis, 1545–1565*
Diarmaid MacCulloch *The Later Reformation in England, 1547–1603*
Keith Perry *British Politics and the American Revolution*
A. J. Pollard *The Wars of the Roses*
David Powell *British Politics and the Labour Question, 1868–1990*
Michael Prestwich *English Politics in the Thirteenth Century*
G. R. Searle *The Liberal Party: Triumph and Disintegration, 1886–1929*
Paul Seaward *The Restoration, 1660–1668*
Robert Stewart *Party and Politics, 1830–1852*
John W. Young *Britain and European Unity since 1945*

FORTHCOMING TITLES

Rodney Barker *Politics, Peoples and Government*
A. D. Carr *Medieval Wales*
Peter Catterall *The Labour Party, 1918–1940*
David Childs *Britain since 1939*
Eveline Cruickshanks *The Glorious Revolution*
Anne Curry *The Hundred Years' War*
John Davis *British Politics, 1885–1931*
David Dean *Parliament and Politics in Elizabethan and
Jacobean England, 1558–1614*
Susan Doran *English Foreign Policy in the Sixteenth Century*
David Eastwood *England, 1750–1850: Government and Community in
the Provinces*
Brian Golding *The Normans in England 1066–1100:
Conquest and Colonisation*
Steven Gunn *Early Tudor Government, 1485–1558*
Angus Hawkins *British Party Politics, 1852–1886*
Alan Heesom *The Anglo-Irish Union, 1800–1922*
Hiram Morgan *Ireland in the Early Modern Periphery, 1534–1690*
Bruce Webster *Scotland in the Middle Ages*
Ann Williams *Kingship and Government in pre-Conquest England*

Please also note that a sister series, *Social History in Perspective*, is now
available; it covers the key topics in social, cultural and religious history.

THE LABOUR PARTY
SINCE 1945

KEVIN JEFFERYS

150th YEAR

M

MACMILLAN

© Kevin Jefferys 1993

All rights reserved. No reproduction, copy or transmission of
this publication may be made without written permission.

No paragraph of this publication may be reproduced, copied or
transmitted save with written permission or in accordance with
the provisions of the Copyright, Designs and Patents Act 1988,
or under the terms of any licence permitting limited copying
issued by the Copyright Licensing Agency, 90 Tottenham Court
Road, London W1P 9HE.

Any person who does any unauthorised act in relation to this
publication may be liable to criminal prosecution and civil
claims for damages.

First published 1993 by
THE MACMILLAN PRESS LTD
Houndmills, Basingstoke, Hampshire RG21 2XS
and London
Companies and representatives
throughout the world

ISBN 0–333–52974–X hardcover
ISBN 0–333–52975–8 paperback

A catalogue record for this book is available
from the British Library

Printed in Hong Kong

Series Standing Order

If you would like to receive future titles in this series as they are
published, you can make use of our standing order facility. To
place a standing order please contact your bookseller or, in case
of difficulty, write to us at the address below with your name
and address and the name of the series. Please state with which
title you wish to begin your standing order. (If you live outside
the United Kingdom we may not have the rights in your area, in
which case we will forward your order to the publisher concerned.)

Customer Services Department, Macmillan Distribution Ltd.
Houndmills, Basingstoke, Hampshire RG21 2XS, England.

Every effort has been made to trace all copyright-holders but
if any have been inadvertently overlooked, the publishers will
be pleased to make any necessary arrangement at the
first opportunity.

For Peter and Joy

CONTENTS

Introduction   1

1 **Labour's Finest Hour, 1945–51**   8

2 **Years of Opposition, 1951–64**   35

3 **The Wilson Governments, 1964–70**   60

4 **'Crisis. What Crisis?', 1970–79**   82

5 **The End of the Road?, 1979–92**   106

Conclusion   130

Notes   136

Select Bibliography   151

Index   158

INTRODUCTION

The Labour party dominated British politics in 1945. As the Second World War drew to a close in Europe, the coalition government of Conservative and Labour forces which had governed Britain since 1940 broke apart. Winston Churchill, the nation's inspirational wartime Prime Minister, called upon the electorate to return him as the head of a new Conservative administration, arguing that he alone could tackle the legacy of six years of war against Nazi Germany. Among politicians and commentators, it was widely anticipated that Churchill would sweep back to power in the general election of July 1945, just as Lloyd George had triumphed in 1918 as the 'man who won the war'. But this prediction proved to be wildly inaccurate. As the election results filtered through, it became apparent that Labour had won a landslide victory. At the last pre-war election, held in 1935, Labour trailed the Tory-dominated National government by 200 parliamentary seats. In 1945, however, Labour secured nearly half the popular vote, winning 393 seats, compared with 210 for the Conservatives. Hence it was not Churchill but the relatively unknown Labour leader, Clement Attlee, who went to Buckingham Palace to accept the royal invitation to form Britain's post-war government. 'We', one Labour MP was reputed to have shouted at his opponents across the floor of the newly-assembled House of Commons, 'are the masters now'.[1] And yet Labour was not to remain 'the master' for long. By 1951 Churchill was back in Downing Street, marking the onset of what many regard as the Labour party's steady decline as an electoral force. As Table 1 illustrates, after being in office for much of the 1960s and 1970s, Labour support slumped disastrously: 1979 was the first of four successive election defeats, with the party barely able to average 35

1

per cent of the total votes cast. The tide that had swept Labour to power in 1945 had not just receded; it had disappeared out of sight.

TABLE 1   *British general election results, 1945–92*[*]

	Conservative	Labour	Liberal	Alliance		
1945	210	393	12		Lab majority	147
1950	298	315	9		Lab majority	6
1951	321	295	6		Con majority	17
1955	345	277	6		Con majority	59
1959	365	258	6		Con majority	100
1964	304	317	9		Lab majority	4
1966	253	364	12		Lab majority	96
1970	330	288	6		Con majority	30
1974 [Feb.]	297	301	14		Minority Lab govt.	
1974 [Oct.]	277	319	13		Lab majority	3
1979	339	269	11		Con majority	44
1983	397	209		23	Con majority	144
1987	376	229		22	Con majority	102
1992	336	271	20 [Lib Dems]		Con majority	21

[*] 'Minor' parties not included

Why then did the party that governed for half of the period between 1945 and 1979 falter so badly in the 1980s? This question has preoccupied the many commentators and observers of post-war Labour politics. In future years, as a broader range of evidence becomes available for the study of British politics since the 1960s, the debate about 'Labour decline' may well come to echo that inspired by George Dangerfield's book on *The Strange Death of Liberal England*. Controversy among historians of electoral change in early twentieth-century Britain has tended to revolve around whether the demise of Asquith's Liberal party should be seen as the inevitable product of a developing class-based society or the accidental result of policy failures, personality clashes and unforeseen external events such as war. The same tests might be applied to Labour since the Second World War. How far, to employ Peter Clarke's terminology, should the party's difficulties be attributed to 'structural' factors that operated outside individual control? Was Labour primarily the victim, for example, of improvements in living standards that transformed the pre-1945 class structure? Or should greater weight be given to 'contingent' or unpredictable explanations of Labour's decline? These might include the impact of personal and ideological divisions within party ranks or the failings of leadership associated particularly with Harold Wilson and Jim Callaghan.[2] As yet, there have been few attempts to synthesise the various contributions to the debate made by contemporary historians, political scientists and journalists.[3] The initial aim of this book is to provide, for the first time, an overview of the whole period between 1945 and 1992 in order to assess when and how 'the strange death of Labour Britain' came about.

But to focus exclusively on the issue of electoral decline would provide an incomplete picture of Labour since 1945. It would also be an injustice to those who have shed light on numerous important aspects of the party's recent history: on Labour's domestic and international policy in office; on links with the trade union movement; on party organisation or ideology; and on the party's role in local as well as national politics.[4] Although some of these themes can only be touched upon briefly in a study of this length, the controversies generated do have a central place in the chapters that follow. What were the main achievements, for instance, of Attlee's 1945–51 government? Was the Prime Minister right to describe his record at home and abroad as constituting a 'revolution without tears', or was this a lost opportunity for a more fundamental transformation of British society? How far did Labour really become a party of 'revisionism' in opposition between 1951 and 1964, and what was the legacy of internal division during these years? Why was Harold Wilson unable to deliver on his promise of a 'technological revolution' after 1964, and how far were his economic failings balanced by success in social policy? To what extent did Labour's close relationship with the unions lie at the heart of the chronic economic malaise of the 1970s? And to what extent did the long period of opposition after 1979 produce a genuinely reformed party, both in terms of programme and procedures? The second aim of this book is therefore to give some sense of the development of the Labour movement in the round since the war. The conclusion, finally, will provide a means of drawing together discussion of the various influences that have dictated Labour's fortunes. In order to achieve these aims, it is first necessary to look – if only fleetingly – at pre-war British politics, for it was during its infancy that much of the character of party that came to power in 1945 was determined.

Labour had only emerged as a distinct political force around the turn of the century, and for many years made little impression on the two dominant groups in Edwardian politics, the Conservatives and the Liberal party. Before the First World War the Labour party, as it officially became known in 1906, was primarily a working-class pressure group. In an effort to protect workers' interests by securing greater parliamentary representation, leading trade unionists decided to ally themselves with socialist societies such as the Independent Labour Party – the original home of many senior ministers in the 1945 government, including Attlee. It was this marriage of forces that prompted Ernest Bevin's pertinent, though unfortunate, comment that the party was born 'out of the bowels' of the trade unions. Historians have long been divided over the extent to which the rise of Labour can be traced back before 1914, though it is generally agreed that the new Labour alliance – of socialists and trade unionists – faced many teething problems. In competing for votes under the restricted pre-war franchise, any limited parliamentary successes were the product of an electoral arrangement with the Liberals, and the small band of Labour MPs at Westminster were distinguishable from progressive Liberals more in terms of humble social background than political philosophy. On the other hand, the seeds of future Labour success could be seen in rapidly growing union support, bringing greatly increased financial resources and and a growing identification of Labour as the natural party of the working classes.[5]

The Great War led to a critical breakthrough. Asquith's Liberal government came under increasing pressure in meeting the demands of total war, and gradually after 1916 Liberal forces became polarised between followers of Asquith and his replacement as Prime Minister, Lloyd George. The carnage on the Western front placed immense strain on all the political parties, but building from a lower base Labour was suddenly presented with fresh opportunities. In 1918 a new constitution and organisational structure was adopted – with lasting consequences for the party's future development. Henceforth Labour was pledged in theory to 'Clause Four Socialism', with its commitment to securing the 'common ownership of the means of production, distribution and exchange'. In practice, the trade unions retained a prominent place within the party's federal structure, and helped to ensure that Labour's dominant strand of thinking was a reformist or 'labourist' ideology that sought gradual social and economic change rather than the overthrow of capitalism. Above all, the 1918 constitution was a symbolic reflection of Labour's new-found confidence. With the Liberals in disarray, the party was well placed to benefit from a massive extension of the franchise after the war, and finally severed any lingering ties with local Liberal forces. Labour's strength, as it had been before the war, was still confined to the industrial heartlands of Britain – in northern England, Scotland and south Wales – but by the early 1920s Liberalism had lost its claim to be the established party of the left in British politics. In 1924 the arrival of a new force on the national stage was confirmed when Ramsay MacDonald went to Downing Street to form the first Labour government.[6]

The experience of 1924 was not, however, a happy one. As head of a minority administration, dependent upon Liberal support in the House of Commons, MacDonald had few ambitions beyond demonstrating that Labour was 'fit to govern'. In terms of electoral strategy and party organisation, MacDonald proved an effective leader, but the first Labour government had little to show in the way of legislative success before a further election returned the Conservatives to power. Nor did MacDonald fare any better in domestic policy when Labour increased its share of the vote sufficiently to form a second minority government in 1929. The paucity of serious thinking on economic issues was now exposed as a severe recession took hold, deepened by the effects of the Wall Street Crash in the United States. Labour's cautious and economically orthodox Chancellor, Philip Snowden, was power-less to prevent a steep rise in unemployment, and in 1931 the cabinet split openly over proposed cuts in unemployment benefit. MacDonald defected to form a new 'National' administration, including Conservatives and many Liberals, leaving his former colleagues to stand condemned for their inept handling of the economic crisis. In the subsequent general election, the party was reduced to a rump of only 46 MPs. The crisis of 1931 subsequently entered Labour mythology as the year of MacDonald's 'betrayal'; at the same time, it had cruelly highlighted the limitations of the formative Labour movement, both in terms of a lack of imaginative leadership and a failure to devise coherent and sustainable policies.

But the debacle of 1931 did, in the longer-term, open up a new phase in the party's history. Against the backcloth of the 'hungry thirties', pressure from the Labour left for more direct attacks on the capitalist system was gradually contained. Both the political and industrial wings of the movement continued to be dominated by men of less militant persuasion. Although regarded initially as a stop-gap figure, part of the reason for Attlee's emergence as party leader in 1935 was that he shared a broad concern with pragmatic reform, rather than with what was widely seen as the unworkable theorising of the left. Hence the new leadership presided over a gradual redefinition of domestic policy, inspired by a group of mostly younger economists who evolved a form of democratic socialism which combined demand management with nationalisation and physical planning. The result was *Labour's Immediate Programme* of 1937, a radical policy document which called for wide-ranging state intervention to tackle unemployment, together with proposals for social reform that went well beyond prevailing Conservative orthodoxy. This domestic rethink – foreshadowing much of Labour's policy in office after 1945 – was accompanied by a new realism in foreign affairs. After Hitler's rise to power in Germany, the Labour movement slowly moved away from its traditional quasi-pacifism. The party became increasingly hostile to the appeasement of the fascist dictators practised by the Prime Minister after 1937, Neville Chamberlain. Although personal antipathy towards Chamberlain led Labour leaders to decline his offer of coalition once war had broken out, there was no doubt that party followers throughout the country would support the fight against Nazism.[7]

By September 1939 the Labour party thus looked to have become once more a credible party of government. But there were still few signs that the electorate had lost faith with Chamberlain, or that Labour was capable of breaking out of its traditional working-class strongholds. The experience of the Second World War changed all this, and provided the backcloth to the 1945 election victory. After Chamberlain fell from power in May 1940 – the result of frustration with early British setbacks in the war – there was a pronounced swing to the left in public opinion, though this was masked at the time by the suspension of normal political activity and by Churchill's immense popularity as war leader. Underpinning the shift in opinion as the war progressed was an egalitarian ethic which followed on from the mobilisation of the entire civilian population and from the intense physical dangers of life in the Blitz. If the Great War of 1914–18 had been fought for King and Country, then the conflict against Hitler soon came to be seen as a 'People's War'.[8] After the 'turn of the tide' on the battlefield late in 1942, when the defeat of Nazism could for the first time be seriously contemplated, Labour also benefited from a growing interest in welfare reform. Indicators of public feeling showed a marked anti-Tory trend, exacerbated by the Prime Minister's cool response to the Beveridge Report on social security and other proposals for social change. By concentrating so exclusively on the war effort, Churchill clearly misjudged the desire of the British people to create a 'New Jerusalem' – a theme made central in Labour's election campaign at the end of the war.[9] The popular enthusiasm for Attlee's brand of corporate socialism evident in 1945 allowed Labour to come to power in circumstances markedly different from those that attended the earlier Mac-Donald administrations. The noisy singing and cheering that accompanied the new Prime Minister as he returned from Buckingham Palace to begin his premiership was indicative of a remarkable transformation in British politics. For the first time in its history, Labour was fully prepared for power. Friends and enemies alike had no notion of imminent decline; in the summer of 1945 party activists were convinced that the forward march of Labour was irresistible.

1

LABOUR'S FINEST HOUR, 1945–51

I

The post-war Labour governments left a profound mark on modern Britain. After the landslide election victory of 1945, Attlee's government wasted no time in launching a series of major policy initiatives. In domestic politics, attention centred on two themes. By 1947 the nation's pre-war market economy had become a mixture of private and publicly-owned industries, following the government's extensive programme of nationalisation. Alongside this mixed economy, legislation was soon passed confirming the establishment of a welfare state. Labour, as it never tired of reminding voters at subsequent elections, was the party that had introduced both the national health service and a new system of social security, designed to enshrine the Beveridge principle of protection for all 'from the cradle to the grave'. By the time Attlee's second, short-lived government of 1950–51 left office, Labour could claim much of the credit for the creation of a new order: a 'post-war settlement' that was to remain in place for a generation to come. In overseas policy, the legacy of these years was equally far-reaching. In retrospect, British withdrawal from India was to mark the first step in a transition from Empire to Commonwealth. And during the early stages of the Cold War between the superpowers, the United States and the Soviet Union, Labour's Foreign Secretary, Ernest Bevin, played a pivotal role in re-ordering international affairs. Most notably, as the 'iron curtain' descended across Europe, he helped to place on a more secure basis Britain's wartime alliance with the Americans; a process culminating in the formation of the North Atlantic Treaty Organisation (NATO) in 1949. Abroad, as much as at home, the years after 1945 saw the initiation of trends that were to dominate political development in the decades that followed.

Most historians therefore agree that the post-war Labour government was amongst the most influential in twentieth-century politics. But assessments of the end result have been varied. During the 1980s, when attempts were made to break with much of the post-war settlement, the 1945 government came under fierce attack. According to those on the political right, Britain took a 'wrong-turning' in the aftermath of war; in particular, it was alleged, the powers of the state were extended too far, helping to create levels of social provision that would be unsustainable in the long-term.[1] The most detailed research on the Attlee governments, however, has been carried out by historians of the left. For some, such as Kenneth Morgan and Henry Pelling, the 1945 government represented the only really successful example as yet of democratic socialism in practice. In the words of Morgan, the achievements of these years brought the Labour movement 'to the zenith of its achievement as a political instrument for humanitarian reform'.[2] Others, though, have been less generous. Many left-wing critics, such as Ralph Miliband and John Saville, see the period as one of wasted opportunity. Instead of a socialist transformation, fulfilling the hopes of 1945, Labour offered only cautious change, involving little redistribution of wealth at home, and a foreign policy that tied Britain to the militantly capitalist United States (USA).[3] This chapter, by reviewing first the circumstances in which Labour came to power and then the unfolding of policy after 1945, will emphasise the cohesiveness of the party and the successes rather than the failings of Attlee's ministers. When set against the standard of previous governments, and in view of the legacy left by six years of total war, the 1945 administration could boast two remarkable achievements: at home it created a fairer society, and abroad it made Britain more secure as an international power. With the benefit of hindsight, this was to be Labour's 'finest hour'.

II

The Attlee years, with one or two exceptions, were to be characterised by strong leadership and by unprecedented unity at all levels of the Labour movement. One of the ironies of this was that, at first sight, Clement Attlee did not strike observers as a strong leader. The aloof, enigmatic Attlee, according to his detractors, was 'a modest man with much to be modest about'. As Peter Hennessy has noted, on the 'equivalent of the Richter scale for oratory, the needle scarcely flickered'.[4] In reality, however, Attlee's inner confidence – the product of his middle-class background and public school training – grew as he showed himself to be a brisk and effective co-ordinator of government business. If he lacked charisma, then as far as rank-and-file activists were concerned, this was more than made up by integrity and loyalty to the party's principles. As those who worked closely with him acknowledged, the Prime Minister's combination of 'honesty, common sense and intelligence' made him the ideal foil for the powerful personalities around the cabinet table.[5] Aside from a brief period in 1947, Attlee's leadership went unchallenged. In part this was due to the unswerving loyalty of the Foreign Secretary, Ernest Bevin. A further irony here was that Bevin was far from being traditional Foreign Office material. The semi-literate son of a farm labourer, he was a no-nonsense figure who had made his reputation as Britain's most powerful trade union leader between the wars. Bevin, according to some colleagues, was the toughest statesman Labour had yet produced; someone who as Minister of Labour during the war showed himself quite willing to give the Tories 'a good kick up the pants'.[6] With his massive physical presence and bullying manner, Bevin was in many ways the strongest personality in the 1945 government, though he was never tempted by suggestions that he might displace the Prime Minister. Rather Attlee and Bevin, both loners in their own ways, developed a relationship that was the closest either had in politics; it was this

10

alliance that was to dominate government proceedings until 1950.

The solidity of the Attlee-Bevin axis proved a source of frustration for a third member of Labour's inner cabinet, Herbert Morrison. As the defeated candidate for the party leadership back in 1935, Morrison continued to believe that he would make a more effective, high-profile leader than Attlee. His preoccupation with internal party affairs led many to dismiss him as a machine politician, the 'chirpy cockney' more concerned with intrigue than with high policy. Morrison was nevertheless to make an invaluable contribution to the 1945 government. Appointed as Lord President of the Council and Leader of the House of Commons, his responsibilities ranged from co-ordinating domestic policy to maintaining the morale and unity of the parliamentary party. He soon became recognised, in the words of one opponent, as 'the Government's handyman'.[7] The two remaining members of Labour's 'big five' were also to have a profound impact on the government's fortunes, though for shorter periods of time. The Chancellor of the Exchequer until the end of 1947 was to be Hugh Dalton, who like Morrison inspired both distrust and admiration amongst his colleagues. Dalton's overbearing manner proved unsettling to friends and opponents alike, and he certainly relished the gossip of everyday Westminster politics. But at the same time, his guiding principles, as one colleague noted, were 'beautifully simple and clear. He was in favour of miners, the young, white men, socialists, New Zealand, Australia and dwellers in Durham and Northumberland. He was against the Germans, reactionaries, the elderly and the rich'.[8] These prejudices helped to ensure, in the early months, both a radical sense of purpose and a style that deliberately insulted the opposition. In personal terms, there could hardly have been a greater contrast between Dalton's style and that of his successor as Chancellor, Sir Stafford Cripps. A teetotaller and vegetarian, whose working day began with a cold bath at four in the morning, Cripps had been identified with the 'extremism' of the Labour left in the 1930s, but during the war had increasingly come to equate socialism with productive efficiency. As other senior figures began to buckle under the strain of high office, it was Cripps who increasingly came to dominate the government's whole political and economic strategy.

Of the remaining twenty members of the cabinet, about half were solid, loyal and experienced party stalwarts. Amongst the few representatives of the Labour left appointed by Attlee, Manny Shinwell and 'Red' Ellen Wilkinson were both to prove cautious and pragmatic ministers.[9] As a result, the most vocal representative of the left in cabinet was to be its youngest member, Aneurin (Nye) Bevan. Although critical of what he saw as the caution of colleagues, Bevan found himself absorbed by his duties as Minister of Health, and he too rarely dissented from government policy before his resignation over health-service charges in 1951. Hence Attlee was blessed with a talented and broadly united cabinet team, though one frequently accused of being elderly in composition. Indeed in the government as a whole, outside the ranks of the cabinet, only three new entrants to the parliamentary party were rewarded with office in 1945; the youngest was Harold Wilson, a civil servant during the war and now appointed to a junior post at the Ministry of Works. The dearth of opportunities for promotion to government office did not cause any major concern in the Parliamentary Labour Party (PLP), in spite of the transformation that came with 260 new back-benchers after the 1945 election. Aside from having served in the war, the new Labour MPs were generally more middle-class and articulate than their pre-war counterparts, and yet there was to be little of the persistent sniping against ministers that had beset the MacDonald administrations back in the 1920s. Part of the reason for this was organisational. Leaders such as Morrison sought to channel back-bench opinion in constructive directions, establishing for example specialist subject groups, though it would be wrong to claim the Attlee years were free of dissent. The so-called 'Keep Left' group were constantly calling for more radical measures, and indeed five MPs were to be expelled from the party, mostly for expressing pro-Soviet attitudes. But there was never any co-ordinated opposition that might endanger the government's large majority. Apart from the imperatives of party management, this record of harmony reflected broad approval of cabinet policy by back-benchers. Attlee was later to describe the 1945 parliament as the most loyal he could remember.[10]

The same loyalty characterised Labour politics outside the

confines of Westminster. Some critics did use the annual conference – theoretically under the 1918 constitution the controlling instrument in policy formation – in order to voice concern, notably over foreign policy. But ministerial defeats were a rarity, and the general tone of proceedings was placid. Similarly, the party's rank-and-file in the constituencies – which expanded rapidly in these years to reach a peak of over 900,000 members – were generally supportive; criticism of ministers did build up after 1950, though not to the alarming degree Labour governments were later to encounter.[11] Part of the reason that support could be effectively mobilised in the country was the benign attitude of the industrial wing of the Labour movement. The proportion of trade-union-sponsored MPs had fallen from 51 per cent of the PLP in 1935 to 31 per cent in 1945.[12] But Attlee's recognition of the importance of the political-industrial alliance, reflected in the composition of his government, helped to ensure for a considerable time the maintenance of harmonious relations. Many of the omens thus looked good for the Prime Minister. He had assembled a talented and united team of ministers, hardened by wartime experience, and he came to power with a detailed programme overwhelmingly endorsed by the electorate. Nor was there much to fear, at least in the short-term, from the Conservatives, demoralised by the election result and sunk for a while in recrimination. In local elections during the autumn, Labour swept the board, winning seats that had been Conservative-controlled since the turn of the century. But there were some clouds on the horizon. For if the Second World War had transformed the domestic political scene, it had also left Britain more clearly at the mercy of world events. After the euphoria of July 1945, sceptics were soon questioning whether the new government might not find itself undermined by circumstances beyond its control.

III

Victory over Hitler had exacted an enormous economic cost. During the course of the Second World War, Britain had lost almost a quarter of its entire national wealth; exports had fallen by two-thirds as industry geared itself up for war production; and Britain had become the world's largest debtor nation, heavily reliant on 'Lend-Lease' financial assistance from the USA. What was worse, after the sudden ending of hostilities in the Far East, America abruptly terminated Lend-Lease, thereby undermining British hopes of a lengthy transition period that would allow a much-needed breathing space. Labour's first task in office was thus to tackle what Lord Keynes, acting as a special adviser at the Treasury, called a 'financial Dunkirk'. The cabinet's response was to send Keynes to Washington in order to negotiate a fresh financial package, though optimism about receiving an interest-free loan soon evaporated, and ministers found themselves inundated with telegrams from the British delegation requesting advice. 'The plethora of telegrams did not always make for clarity', noted one observer. Dalton turned to Bevin at one stage to ask: '"Foreign Secretary, have you got the telegram?" "I've got 'undreds," replied Bevin.'[13] Eventually, in December 1945, the government accepted a loan of nearly four billion dollars, with repayments to be spread over fifty years. But there were some stringent conditions attached, notably the agreement that sterling would become freely convertible into dollars after only a year. British negotiators believed that such a short time span before the resumption of multilateral trading arrangements would place immense pressure on the British economy – a fear that was to be fully borne out in 1947. Nevertheless, the cabinet and the majority of back-benchers believed there was no option but to accept the American loan. Without such assistance, it was recognised, Britain would suffer living standards lower even than in wartime; Labour's ambitious programme would never get off the ground, and the opposition would be able to present biting austerity as the inevitable product of 'socialism'.[14]

The American loan highlighted some of the difficulties facing British foreign policy in the aftermath of war. Indeed during the first phase of the Attlee government Bevin's conduct of overseas affairs was to generate more internal party controversy than domestic policy. For many months after arriving at the Foreign Office, Bevin made little headway as it became clear that the Anglo-American-Soviet wartime alliance was breaking down. Any prospect of 'left speaking to left' disappeared as Stalin moved to establish a series of one-party dictatorships in Eastern Europe. As the 'iron curtain' inexorably came to divide West from East, Bevin reluctantly came to the conclusion that the greatest danger to European stability was no longer Germany but an expansionist Soviet Union.[15] This did not mean, however, that Britain's relations with its other major wartime ally, the United States, ran smoothly from the outset. As the negotiations over financial assistance indicated, there was considerable suspicion in Washington of 'socialism' and of British 'imperialism' on the world stage. In the Middle East, for example, Bevin's fear of antagonising Arab states led him to respond coolly to demands for a new Jewish homeland; an attitude fiercely criticised by the Zionist lobby in the USA.[16] For his part, Bevin's doubts about American reliability were fuelled by the refusal of Congress to collaborate on the development of nuclear weapons. This refusal, together with the assumption that Britain remained a great power – having troops still stationed in all parts of the world – prompted a secret decision by senior ministers to commission an independent nuclear deterrent.[17] It was not until early 1947 that Soviet intransigence – especially over the future of Germany – made the Americans more amenable to Bevin's concept of 'western co-operation'. In the meantime, a group of Labour back-benchers, alarmed by the onset of the Cold War, tabled a critical amendment in the House of Commons calling for 'a democratic and constructive socialist alternative to an otherwise inevitable conflict between American capitalism and Soviet communism'. Bevin, in typically bruising fashion, referred to this as a 'stab in the back', and pointed out that Britain had not sought hostile relations with the Russians; in the event, the amendment was not forced to a division.[18]

In domestic policy, there was much less party anxiety. Conversely, back-benchers were delighted by the speed with which the government introduced its reform programme. The pace was dictated in the early days by the Chancellor, Hugh Dalton, who while recognising the overriding need to recover lost export markets, was determined to 'advance along the road towards economic and social equality'.[19] Hence Dalton's economic policy was characterised by attempts to assist ordinary working families, the majority of whom were still suffering the hardships associated with rationing and war shortages. Food subsidies, for example, were maintained at high levels in order to keep down living costs, and the progressive nature of Dalton's amendments to the taxation system led to loud complaints from the opposition. Perhaps most striking of all was the Chancellor's determination to avoid the type of post-war slump that had so blighted working-class families after the First World War. With the exception of a short period in 1947, unemployment was to remain at far lower levels than between the wars, in spite of the return to the job market of millions of service personnel. This outcome was of course partly dependent upon a revival of world trade after the war, though ministers could claim some of the credit. At the Board of Trade, for instance, Stafford Cripps encouraged a vigorous policy of regional planning. Such an approach helped to ensure that economic recovery rapidly spread to areas blighted in the 1930s, notably the industrial heartlands of northern England and south Wales. This in turn was to have lasting electoral implications. Through the various economic difficulties to come before 1950, Labour's strongest claim on the loyalty of working-class voters was that it had become 'the party of full employment, the party which had exorcised the ghosts of Jarrow, Wigan and Merthyr Tydfil'.[20]

The most distinctive element of the government's economic strategy was its programme of nationalisation. Labour had long been committed to public ownership, both as a means of creating service industries, operated not simply for profit but for the benefit of the whole community, and as a technique for redeeming certain industries such as coal that had proved inefficient in private hands. These claims had a strong appeal in 1945, coming at the end of a war in which the state had assumed much greater responsibility over the national economy. As a result, under the guidance of Herbert Morrison, an extensive programme of nationalisation was rapidly introduced, covering the civil aviation, coal, transport and electricity industries. Although the opposition at first put up only token resistance, as Conservative morale revived so there were increasingly strong attacks on Labour's interference with the free market economy. By the time the government came to take gas into public hands in 1948, much of the early confidence about the beneficial effects of nationalisation was evaporating, and Hugh Gaitskell, attempting to pilot the legislation through the Commons, became so provoked by one of the 800 wrecking amendments tabled by the Conservatives that he compared his opponents to Hitler. In the meantime, much of Labour's policy, including the public corporation form of management adopted for the nationalised industries, reflected a desire to conciliate the trade union movement. The natural sympathy of many union leaders to the Attlee government was reinforced early on when the cabinet moved to repeal the hated Trades Disputes Act of 1927 – a move resisted by Churchill during wartime under pressure from Tory back-benchers. In return for relaxing restrictions on secondary industrial action, union leaders took a lead in urging wage restraint on their members. The new legislation thus confirmed the existence of a mixed and corporate economy in a form that could not have been guaranteed under a Conservative administration.[21]

In social policy, the government's record was a mixture of consolidation and innovation. One of Labour's early priorities was to provide the political will necessary to introduce a new system of social security. This was done by the passage of the National Insurance Act in 1946, piloted through the Commons by Welshman James Griffiths, who had been prominent in refining the party's policy during the war. The new measure was based on the principle of universality, in place of pre-war selectivity, and brought together for the first time a comprehensive range of benefits to provide insurance against sickness, unemployment and old age. Although partisan controversy on this topic was limited in 1946, there were still indications that the Tories hoped to remodel the Beveridge idea in what Churchill had called a 'non-socialist' direction. While the problem of maintaining the level of benefits in the face of rising inflation proved more difficult than anticipated, Labour propagandists could nevertheless subsequently claim that their action had helped to eradicate the most abject poverty of the 1930s.[22] Education was a second area where Labour ministers were generally content to develop lines of policy aleady mapped out before 1945. In particular Ellen Wilkinson and her successor as education minister, George Tomlinson, sought to implement the main proposals of the 1944 Education Act, an agreed wartime measure enshrining the principle that, for the first time, all children over the age of eleven should receive free secondary schooling. An increasingly vocal minority of party opinion believed that genuine equality of opportunity would be impossible if children were divided, in the main, between grammar and secondary modern schools. But as the new school system became operational, ministers hoped that 'parity of esteem' would be attainable, and in the meantime emphasis was placed on short-term objectives. The school-leaving age, for example, was raised to fifteen, and in spite of growing concern about public expenditure, increased Treasury funds were still secured for education, notably to update school buildings suffering from war damage and years of neglect.[23]

The most radical of Labour's social policies, however, were associated with the Minister of Health, Aneurin Bevan. His department still combined responsibility for both health and housing, and there was no doubt that the government's housing programme got off to a poor start. With a population enlarged by a million now crowded into 700,000 fewer properties, owing to wartime damage or destruction, Bevan ran up against a host of difficulties, not least that of obtaining adequate raw materials for the building of new homes. But by 1947 the position was improving, and Bevan's objectives became clearer. In a deliberate attempt to favour working-class families, attention was shifted from private house-building – the priority of the 1930s – towards the local authority rented sector. Four out of five houses built under the Attlee government were to be council properties, constructed to more generous specifications than before the war.[24] The minister eventually came to have a defensible record. Over a million homes were built in the six years after the war, and if there was disappointment about the initial pace of reform, then part of the reason for this was the priority accorded to what the became the jewel in Labour's welfare crown – the National Health Service (NHS). Medical reform had been exhaustively discussed by Churchill's coalition, but party and professional opinion remained divided over the best way forward, and within weeks of coming to office Bevan indicated his determination to go beyond wartime proposals. In particular, he aimed at a stroke to bring the fee-paying, 'voluntary' hospitals into one state system – a move strongly opposed by the Conservative party. Reform of the hospitals thus became a central plank of the 1946 National Health Service Act, which also introduced for the first time free access to general practitioner treatment and to local authority services such as maternity care. The act was enthusiastically endorsed by Labour MPs, though the minister was not without his critics. At one extreme the Socialist Medical Association condemned the failure to introduce a state-salaried general practitioner service; at the other, the British Medical Association was bitterly hostile, and the Tories used their attachment to voluntary hospitals as a pretext for voting against the legislation. But Bevan's achievement remained beyond question. The NHS was to be the most popular, and the most enduring, of Labour's welfare reforms.[25] Labour ministers could reflect with pride on their early months in office. For Hugh Dalton, 1946 was the party's 'Annus Mirabilis'. But the Chancellor was soon to discover how quickly fortunes can change in politics. After the successes of 1946, the following year was to witness a series of crises that pushed the government increasingly on the defensive.

IV

The government's honeymoon period came to an abrupt end owing to a mixture of external factors, over which individuals had little control, and incompetence on the part of senior ministers. Nowhere was this more evident than in the case of the 'winter crisis' early in 1947: a fuel shortage compounded by the severest spell of cold weather for over fifty years. With innumerable villages cut off and the government resorting to emergency measures such as electricity restrictions, it was not long before fingers of accusation were being pointed at the Minister of Fuel and Power, Emanuel Shinwell. Conservative propagandists, eager to point out that the minister had placed too much faith in productivity gains in the coal industry that never materialised, coined the popular slogan 'Shiver with Shinwell'.[26] Aside from being what Hugh Dalton called 'the first really heavy blow to confidence in the Government', later estimates pointed to a 25 per cent loss of industrial output, which in turn cost the nation 200 million pounds in lost exports.[27] This blow to the stimulation of export growth was compounded in the summer by a more serious economic crisis. Britain's deteriorating balance-of-payments position, stemming from a trade imbalance that left the USA in a dominant export position after the war, was adversely affected by the imposition of the so-called 'convertibility clause' attached to the American loan. The free convertibility of pounds into dollars caused havoc on the foreign exchanges, and with sterling under intense pressure, the Chancellor was forced to take drastic action. Dalton recognised that the suspension of convertibility was a humiliation from which his reputation was unlikely to recover, especially as he was forced to follow it up with an austere budget that heralded a new era of counter-inflationary devices. Unlike Shinwell, the Chancellor had tried to warn colleagues in advance that the government was heading 'towards the rapids'; in many ways the convertibility crisis was the unavoidable consequence of the American loan.[28] But in the search for scapegoats, Dalton was clearly left carrying the can, as became clear when the convertibility crisis was unexpectedly followed by a political crisis – by nothing less than an attempt to remove the Prime Minister.

The principal mover in the attempted 'palace revolution' against Attlee was Sir Stafford Cripps, the only senior minister whose reputation grew during the difficult days of 1947. As President of the Board of Trade, Cripps came to believe that the economy would only be revived by stronger leadership than the Prime Minister seemed to offer. He thus approached Dalton and Morrison in order to enlist their support for a plan to replace Attlee with Ernest Bevin, whose background gave him unique experience of both domestic and foreign policy. The Chancellor was tempted by this suggestion, and indeed floated the idea to Bevin himself, only to be met with a blunt rejection. Despite the lack of any firm support, Cripps nevertheless decided to go ahead alone. On 9 September, he boldly confronted the Prime Minister. In a masterfully cool response, Attlee telephoned Bevin to confirm that he had no desire to succeed as leader, and then – without any hint of embarrassment – offered Cripps a new position as Minister of Economic Affairs charged with bringing greater co-ordination to government policy. Having received Cripps as a rebel, the Prime Minister sent him out within minutes as his right-hand man.[29] Attlee did not forget, moreover, that his Chancellor had been an accessory to conspiracy. Shortly before delivering his emergency budget in November 1947, Dalton revealed details to a lobby correspondent in breach of parliamentary convention. Within days, the Chancellor had resigned, to be replaced by Cripps. Attlee later claimed that he accepted the resignation as a matter of principle, though many ministers in the past had survived far graver offences. For Dalton, resignation from high office marked the culmination of Labour's 'Annus Horrendus'. In the wake of recurrent economic difficulties, ministers were faced with a sudden erosion of public confidence; by the autumn the Tories had edged ahead in the opinion polls for the first time since Attlee came to power. In domestic politics, 1947 thus marked an important point of transition: from the confidence of the early months in power to a new, less buoyant phase under a Chancellor who had fewer qualms about tightening the belt.

This pattern was not, however, mirrored in overseas policy. Until the middle of 1947, the Foreign Secretary could point to few tangible results from his endeavours. But over the next two years, his policy produced a series of diplomatic triumphs. It was Bevin, for example, who seized the opportunity of 'Marshall Aid' to establish a new infrastruture for European economic recovery. In the short-term, this helped to ensure a massive injection of American capital: twelve billion dollars came to Europe by 1951, a significant proportion helping to stabilise the British economy after the crises of 1947.[30] Bevin next sought to extend the American commitment in Europe from the economic to the military sphere. His efforts were facilitated by the increasingly bitter atmosphere of the Cold War. Above all, the Berlin blockade, when the Soviet Union cut off access by land to the western sectors of Berlin for over a year, persuaded Congress of the need to abandon its traditional isolationism. As a result, the USA became one of the signatories of a new North Atlantic defence treaty in April 1949. The establishment of NATO, which marked the culmination of Bevin's diplomatic efforts, was broadly welcomed by British political opinion, though a minority of Labour MPs remained implacably opposed, both to the idea of 'subservience' to the USA and to the minister's belligerent anti-communism. To his critics, Bevin retorted that he did not need lessons in democratic socialism from those who held up Stalin as a model, and he recollected that faint-heartedness was associated with appeasement – a policy attacked by the left for failing to produce the type of security Bevin had now delivered. As far as the Empire was concerned, the government's record was more mixed. British withdrawal from both Palestine and India suggested that decolonisation consisted more of unplanned breakdowns than an orderly retreat.[31] Nevertheless, the independence of India did help to establish notions of a new and more flexible Commonwealth. In imperial policy, as in relations with the superpowers, Labour could point to some solid achievements at a time when problems on the home front were intensifying.

Labour's domestic policy clearly became more pragmatic after the crises of 1947. The period between 1948 and the general election in 1950 became indelibly associated in the public mind with restrictions and hardships, a time when ministers used the language of restraint and 'consolidation'. This 'age of austerity' was also closely identified with the figure of the new Chancellor. Sir 'Austere Cripps', as his detractors called him, was notorious for a prodigious work rate that included three hours at his desk before breakfast. Hoping for similar self-discipline from the nation, Cripps believed there was no option other than to continue controlling the consumption of basic foodstuffs, a policy which he presented in the collectivist rhetoric of 'fair shares'.[32] But he was far from being dogmatically committed to the range of government controls over the ecomony bequeathed by the war. Indeed in late 1948 the youthful Harold Wilson, who replaced Cripps at the Board of Trade, was encouraged to announce a 'bonfire of controls'. In practice, Cripps was driven by the belief that only with substantial increases in productivity could Britain maintain its living standards and become a progressively fairer society. The government's line on controls – which employers and trade unions saw as a hindrance to the recovery of export markets – was itself only part of a broader abandonment of 'economic planning'.[33] Doubts about the value of public ownership intensified as the newly nationalised industries came under attack for alleged lack of profitability and poor industrial relations. Resistance to legislation on iron and steel, finally introduced in 1948, was such that ministers became lukewarm about drawing up a new shopping list to extend public ownership. There was little discussion about how nationalisation served the wider needs of the economy, and no attempts were made to impose new controls over private industry. Much to the annoyance of the Labour left, the idea of socialist planning was quietly abandoned in preference for demand management by fiscal and budgetary means, though the extent to which a 'Keynesian revolution' had occurred remains questionable.[34]

In the short-term, the firm resolve of the Chancellor appeared to be paying off. His concentration on exports, for example, helped to greatly reduce the balance of payments deficit. But in the summer of 1949 an economic downturn in the USA was followed by another 'dollar drain' from Britain; as sterling fell on the foreign exchanges, parallels were soon being drawn with 1947. Cripps, like his predecessor, suffered under the strain of events, and had to retire temporarily to a Swiss sanitorium after falling ill. In his absence, the cabinet was persuaded that the only viable means of boosting Britain's reserves was to devalue the pound. Despite fears that this would be seen as a sign of failure on the international stage, Cripps wearily agreed from his sick-bed to a 30 per cent devaluation. Critics argued that the scale of the change was greater than necessary, but party opinion generally accepted that firm action was unavoidable, and by the end of the year economic indicators were again moving in the right direction.[35] The short-lived devaluation crisis did, however, reinforce another policy refinement after 1947 – a more cautious approach to welfare expenditure. Treasury officials had taken the lead in arguing that devaluation would only be effective if accompanied by fresh austerity measures on the home front. This line was fiercely opposed by Nye Bevan and by Hugh Dalton, who having returned to the cabinet as Chancellor of the Duchy of Lancaster, argued that welfare reform should not simply be discharged as ballast whenever the economy hit rough water. After some acrimonious exhanges, the Chancellor had to settle for savings of 120 million pounds, including minor economies in defence, a cutback in the housing programme and a ceiling on future food subsidies.[36]

It was not only external, economic forces that dictated a change in government style after 1947. On the home front, Labour was faced with an increasingly revitalised parliamentary opposition, especially as the Conservatives were able to exploit a populist theme – scarcities and shortages, it was alleged, were all due to socialist 'bureaucracy' and 'inefficiency'. The effectiveness of the Tory revival should not be exaggerated, but it was clearly a further constraint as ministers began to prepare for a general election, eventually called in February 1950.[37] Unlike 1945, Labour's campaign looked as much to the past as to the future. Allegations that the post-war settlement would be threatened by the return of Churchill were strenuously denied by the Conservatives, who emphasised their broad acceptance of welfare reform. In these circumstances, with party divisions less acute, campaigning in the constituencies remained low key. A record turnout helped to ensure that Labour polled more votes than it had in 1945. But so too did the Conservatives. The results revealed a swing across the country of 2.9 per cent against the government, leaving Labour with a majority of just six seats in the House of Commons. Aside from the redrawing of constituency boundaries, which was estimated to have cost the government thirty seats, the regional pattern of results offered the clearest explanation of this narrow victory. Broadly working-class constituencies, especially in the north and west, remained solidly behind the government. But Labour lost ground in seats with a preponderance of middle-class voters, notably in the suburban districts of London and the Home Counties.[38] Looking back on the 1950 election, many on the Labour side believed that austerity was the primary cause of voters' disaffection. 'We proclaimed a just policy of fair shares', reflected Hugh Dalton, 'but the complaint was not so much that shares were unfair, but that they were too small'.[39] Others, more critical, were inclined to blame the government's alleged betrayal of socialist principles. But if the post-1947 'retreat to consensus' had blurred old party distinctions, it had not undermined the essence of the government's achievement. Increased numbers of Labour voters in 1950 reflected the comfort drawn by working people from both full employment and the introduction of welfare reforms. The Cripps era, we might conclude, had not betrayed the hopes of 1945; its main failing was rather that it offered little that was new or exciting for the future. Under the pressure of events, ministers had increasingly focused on the defence rather the development of the post-war settlement, a tendency that was to be reinforced by the narrowness of the election victory in 1950. This time, unlike 1945, there were no joyous celebrations in the streets.

V

With hindsight, the second Attlee administration looked doomed from the outset. Certainly the cabinet – which contained most of the same faces as before – was acutely conscious of the constraints imposed by a tiny parliamentary majority. Hugh Dalton described the election result as the worst of all possible outcomes, leaving Labour in office but 'without authority or power'; most of his colleagues doubted if the government could survive for more than six months.[40] In the short-term, however, Labour fared surprisingly well. Above all, this was due to an economic upturn in 1950 that enabled Britain to relinquish any reliance on Marshall Aid by the end of the year. With the party still holding marginal seats at by elections, back-benchers also remained in good spirits. Angered by opposition attempts to demoralise ministers by resorting to tiring, all night sessions, Labour MPs closed ranks to make government defeats in the House of Commons a rarity. 'It looks', Churchill lamented, 'as though those bastards can stay in as long as they like'.[41] In practice, the second Attlee administration was only blown off course by an entirely unforeseen external development – the outbreak of the Korean War in June 1950. With memories of appeasement still strong, the cabinet had little hesitation in deciding to send British troops to fight against the Communist forces of North Korea. Initially, a hardline response was supported by Labour's rank-and-file, but as it became clear that the United Nations commitment was not confined to a simple defence of South Korea, MPs became increasingly concerned that Britain was tying itself inextricably to the aims of American foreign policy. Such fears were compounded when in early 1951 ministers committed themselves to a massive increase in defence spending. This decision not only placed an immense strain on the British economy; it also precipitated a split in Labour ranks that was to haunt the party throughout the 1950s.

The problem was partly one of personality. In October 1950 Stafford Cripps resigned through ill-health, and was replaced by his Treasury deputy Hugh Gaitskell, at forty-four the second youngest Chancellor since the turn of the century. Gaitskell's rapid promotion was resented in some quarters, not least by Aneurin Bevan, who believed his success as Minister of Health merited promotion to a senior post. Although, as Bevan contempuously pointed out, Gaitskell was 'young in the Movement', and was as yet little known to party activists outside Westminster, there was no doubt that the new Chancellor was a rising star. His economic expertise and reputation for administrative competence certainly impressed several colleagues who found it difficult to tolerate the more volatile Bevan.[42] Aside from the personal rivalry of two potential future leaders, Gaitskell and Bevan soon found themselves at loggerheads over important policy issues. In particular, the new Chancellor was insistent that increases in the defence budget could only be met if economies were made on domestic spending, including the health service. In drawing up his budget plans for 1951, Gaitskell thus made provision for the imposition of new charges for dentures and spectacles. Bevan, though by now transferred to the Ministry of Labour, repeated his belief that cuts should be made in defence, and raised the stakes by warning in public that he would resign if the government departed from the principle of a free health service. With the Prime Minister absent from crucial discussions in hospital, the cabinet – after several attempts to find a compromise formula – overwhelmingly backed the Chancellor. As a result, Gaitskell went ahead on 10 April to announce health service charges as part of a generally well-received budget. After listening to pleas from colleagues about the likely electoral consequences of a government split, Bevan resigned on 22 April, to be followed by two junior ministers, Harold Wilson and John Freeman. At a series of ill tempered meetings, Bevan made violent accusations against his erstwhile colleagues, accusing

Gaitskell of having followed the example of Snowden as a Labour Chancellor who had sold the pass to the Tories. Press commentators wasted no time in speaking of a 'Bevanite' rupture in the Labour party.[43]

What then was the significance of this first major split in Labour ranks since 1945? Health service charges clearly symbolised an emerging division between left and right about future party strategy. Bevan believed that 'Hugh is a Tory', prepared to abandon socialist idealism for the sake of electoral respectability. Gaitskell, in turn, was convinced that Bevan's 'extremism' could destroy Labour, just as Lloyd George had broken the Liberal party.[44] Each case has subsequently found its supporters. Michael Foot has presented the whole episode as a conspiracy aimed at forcing Bevan's resignation; while Gaitskell's biographer argues that health was only being requested to make the same sacrifice as other spending departments.[45] In personal terms, both men behaved badly. Gaitskell demonstrated a degree of inflexibility that alarmed even his closest supporters, while Bevan's strident language antagonised some of those who sympathised with his case. As one minister obeserved, it was intolerable for cabinet majorities of eighteen to two to be overturned just because Bevan happened to be in the minority. Purely in terms of the issue itself, events were subsequently to bear out much of Bevan's case: as he predicted, cuts in health were unnecessary when production difficulties made it impossible to carry out the full rearmament programme.[46] On the other hand, by forcing events to a head, Bevan cast a shadow over the whole administration. Despite his more temperate language in the months that followed, some of his supporters now launched embarrassing attacks on the government. The Bevanites were still as yet an informal and indistinct alliance of back-benchers, but their demands for industrial democracy and further nationalisation clearly ran counter to Labour's official policy. Back-bench discontent was also enchanced by the economic difficulties facing the government in mid-1951. With a sudden deterioration in the balance of payments, it was difficult for the Chancellor to refute claims that rearmament was undermining Labour's electoral prospects. At the same time, foreign affairs afforded little relief for the government. The immense pressures on Ernest Bevin finally forced his resignation through illness early in 1951; he died shortly afterwards in the midst of the cabinet wrangling over health service charges. The loss of his two most able senior colleagues, Cripps and Bevin, within six months of each other, was a blow from which the Prime Minister found it difficult to recover. Bevin's death certainly underlined the extent to which Attlee had come to rely on his Foreign Secretary. After rejecting the possibility of offering the post to Bevan – whose temper was not improved by again being passed over for high office – Attlee decided that on grounds of seniority the Foreign Office should go to Herbert Morrison. But from the outset Morrison's style and conduct of foreign affairs came in for considerable criticism. He was soon struggling to come to terms with a series of contentious international issues, such as Britain's role in the Middle East and the Korean War, which continued without sign of resolution.[47] Domestic and foreign policy thus combined to leave the impression of an administration that had lost its sense of direction. The Conservative opposition, encouraged by a clear lead in the opinion polls during the autumn of 1951, now intensified its efforts to demoralise Labour with late-night sittings in the Commons. In such circumstances, Attlee's decision to go to the country in October occasioned some surprise, not least amongst his cabinet colleagues. The Prime Minister was swayed, at least in part, by a desire to oblige the King; it would be unfair, Attlee felt, for an election to take place the following spring when George VI was scheduled to visit Australia. As the nation prepared to go to the polls, it was difficult to detect much of the enthusiasm and unity of 1945. In particular, the resignation of Bevan had led to a sense that one of Labour's great pre-war difficulties – of internal division – was returning to bedevil the party.[48]

The 1951 election campaign was fought on similar lines to that of 1950. Labour's emphasis on the consolidation of post-war advances, such as full employment and the welfare state, was repeated, while the Conservative campaign also followed the pattern of the previous year, with Churchill promising to 'set the people free'. With most of the arguments having been extensively rehearsed, attempts to breathe life into the campaign came to little. Conservative efforts to exploit Labour divisions – using slogans such as 'The End is Nye' – were blunted by Bevan speaking out strongly in favour of party unity. Political observers were generally agreed that party differences on domestic policy had narrowed and that the fierce animosity of 1945 was absent; so much so that newspaper reporters had to resort to detailed descriptions of Mrs Attlee's eccentric driving as the Prime Minister busied himself with crossword puzzles in the back of his car on a nationwide tour. The outcome of the election was a further small swing towards the Conservatives, sufficient to allow Churchill to return to Downing Street with a seventeen-seat parliamentary majority. Most of the electorate voted the same way as in 1950. For the crucial minority who did switch allegiance, the main consideration was not Labour's internal divisions, but increases in the cost of living and unsatisfied material ambitions. Over half of the twenty or so Conservative gains were made in the south-east, especially in London suburbs, where Churchill's rallying cry of prosperity and opportunity had its greatest resonance.[49] Labour also suffered from a greatly reduced number of Liberal candidates, compared with 1950. With hindsight, there were many ironies about the 1951 result. Not only did George VI's sudden death compound Attlee's tactical error in calling for an early election; but during 1952 the economy entered a period of rapid growth from which Labour may well have benefited had they remained longer in office.[50] In addition, by again piling up huge majorities in its industrial heartlands, Labour actually won more votes, if fewer seats, than the Conservatives. As a result, some within the party were by no means downcast. Hugh Dalton described the outcome as 'wonderful', believing that the Conservatives would soon run into economic and electoral difficulties.[51] In the event, he was to be profoundly mistaken: most of Labour's generation of 1945 were never again to return to high office.

VI

In looking back on this momentous post-war period, many critics have failed to take adequate account of the historical context in which the Attlee government operated. Those who lament the emphasis given to welfare reform tend to overlook the desire of the

British electorate coming out of the war to see the creation of a 'New Jerusalem'. Labour was elected in 1945 precisely because of its commitment to reforms that ordinary voters felt had been too long denied, and if this meant extending state powers to the level of other advanced industrial nations then this was a price well worth paying. Left-wing critics, by contrast, have argued that there was too little rather than too much socialism during the Attlee years. Britain, it has been noted, remained a profoundly unequal and class-ridden society, in which one per cent of the population still owned 50 per cent of all private capital.[52] Such a critique, however, wrongly presupposes that a more radical agenda was readily available in the late 1940s. In reality, the Labour left was 'uncertain of its aims, confused about methods and weak in numbers'.[53] The Keep Left group of MPs was remarkably imprecise about what 'more socialism' would mean in practice, and it was noticeable that in later years even those who were disaffected at the time came to share the view, still widely held in the Labour movement, that little more could have been achieved in the circumstances. In the words of the veteran left winger Ian Mikardo:

I am proud to have been a member of that postwar generation and to have taken part in the radical changes it wrought, and wrought in the face of the most adverse circumstances and the most crippling handicaps. The 1945–48 period was a time when anyone who looked for excuses to put off tackling a fresh task had no difficulty in finding them. We had sold a lot of our overseas assets to pay for the war effort, and had left ourselves poor and shabby; many of our cities were blighted by large areas of rubble and many of our homes needed urgent repairs; . . . the task of recovery, and even of day-to day existence were hampered by shortages of even basic necessities.

But we were a tough lot in that generation: we didn't look for excuses and we weren't put off by difficulties. . . . The Britons of that generation were prepared, as no nation before had ever been, to bear one another's burdens. . . . In those difficult years we sought to answer, for the first time in the recorded history of man, the first question a man ever asked, Am I my brother's keeper?, and we said Yes, brother, you are your brother's keeper.[54]

Why then have so many in Labour ranks come to regard the Attlee years as something of a golden age? In part this view has developed in response to the sense of disappointment that dogged later Labour governments, but even as Attlee left office in 1951, the party faithful were generally satisfied with what had been achieved. In domestic politics, the government could claim credit for its part in shaping the nation's economic recovery. By emphasising the primacy of investment and increased production, Attlee's cabinet provided a framework for sustained growth. Exports rose threefold; industrial output grew by one-third; and the gross domestic product rose by three per cent per year after 1947. With the aid of the American loan and Marshall Aid, the balance of payments showed current-account surpluses in 1948 and 1950, before the Korean War led to a deficit in 1951. And in spite of rising import costs, consumer prices and wage rates were pegged to average rises of less than five per cent. If this compared favourably with the pre-war period, then so too did the government's success – except in 1947 – in maintaining much lower levels of unemployment. Clearly the resumption of world trade, by releasing suppressed wartime demand, was of prime importance in this context, but it would be wrong not to highlight the imprint left by Labour ministers. Similar circumstances, after all, had produced a short-term boom after the First World War, followed by a deep recession. Careful planning after 1945 helped to ensure first that demobilisation was carried out without upsetting economic recovery, and secondly that there was no return to mass unemployment in the formerly depressed regions of northern and western Britain. Unemployment throughout the north-east coastal region of England in 1938 had been 38 per cent; in June 1951 it was running at 1.5 per cent.[55] The most exhaustive study yet of Labour's economic policy concludes that, notwithstanding the intractability of many features of Britain's 'industrial disease', this was a record that could hardly have been bettered.[56]

Economic recovery was also vital in laying the foundation for

Labour's welfare programme. Again, the record here suggests considerable improvement, in the face of some determined opposition, over pre-war provision. The long list of reforms carried through the House of Commons meant services of a kind that had hitherto been unthinkable for a majority of the population. Apart from a new found employment security, Labour's programme benefited all sections of the community and all age ranges. For the young, free secondary education became a right for the first time; for the elderly, pensions approximated as never before to the level of a living income. Bevan's house-building programme meant that affordable, decent accommodation came within the reach of thousands of lower income families. In addition, the most popular of Labour's reforms, the National Health Service, soon demonstrated its worth by treating millions of patients in its first years of operation, highlighting the pent-up demand that existed within British society for medical services. It may have been the case that equality between the sexes – never seriously on the political agenda in the 1940s – remained as elusive as ever, but working-class women could nevertheless benefit from a range of new services. Free health care provided a striking illustration. One woman later recalled how, on the evening before the health service came into operation in 1948, she was delivered of her baby shortly before midnight. The next morning she was presented with a bill for six pounds by the doctor; had the baby been born fifteen minutes later, there would have been no charge.[57] If much remained to be done to overcome inequalities in British society, party activists were convinced that some important steps had been taken in the right direction, and taken moreover in the face of both economic hardship and political resistance.[58]

Nor did the government need to feel defensive about its achievements on the world stage. These included the forging of the Anglo-American 'special relationship', upon which Western security would henceforth be based, and the initiation of moves towards independence for a sizeable proportion of Britian's colonial population. Subsequent claims that Bevin should have accepted more readily the nation's eclipse as a world power, though easy to make with hindsight, tend to ignore the realities of 1945. In spite of the rise of the superpowers, British military and industrial power at the end of the war inevitably led to caution in reviewing global commitments. As for missing the idea of creating a European 'third force', this understates the legacy of anti-German feeling after 1945, and ignores the fact that only a quarter of Britain's trade in the late 1940s was with continental Europe. Politicians and officials alike had no reason for believing that the Commonwealth and the Sterling Area would soon lose their prominence in trading terms. The idea that Britain had overstretched itself only came to have greater validity in the 1950s, after the economic revival of western Europe became more obvious and events such as Suez highlighted the fragility of the Empire. In the meantime, Bevin's conduct of policy had left Britain a degree of flexibility that would have been envied by foreign policy-makers in the 1930s.[59] This does not mean, of course, that criticisms of Bevin at the time were without foundation. Just as back benchers were anxious that on the home front ministers had not shown how nationalisation contributed to the creation of a socialist commonwealth, so several aspects of foreign policy were regarded as indefensible. In the case, for example, of the government's benign attitude towards South Africa – an important source of uranium for nuclear weapons – one junior minister found himself dismissed and cold-shouldered after criticising the racism of apartheid.

But what of the impact of the Attlee years on the Labour party itself? Here it might be concluded that three inter-connected problems remained unresolved at the time of the 1951 election. In the first place, despite its support among working-class voters, Labour had not been able to retain the loyalty of many within the middle-class who had backed the party in 1945. This was essential if the Conservatives were again to be dislodged from power, and was closely linked with a second anxiety. The successful implementation of Labour's traditional programme of corporate socialism left an obvious problem: what was to be the party's new vision of the future? In facing this, tactical questions inevitably became entangled with issues of ideology and principle. For the likes of Morrison, consolidation of gains made since 1945 was the essential priority; moderation, he argued, was essential in order to keep on board many voters whose concern was not with the fading wartime ethos of fair shares, but with material affluence. Many other activists, however, believed that consolidation on its own was insufficient for a party committed to radical change. This problem, of how to construct a new programme appropriate for the 1950s, was itself linked with a third difficulty: that of the age profile of the party leadership. Senior ministers who dominated cabinet proceedings were all members of the same, by now ageing, political generation, unable to provide the innovative thinking required to reinvigorate Labour policy. The authority of the 'big five' had, in the short term, been the foundation of Labour's achievements after 1945; but by making promotion from the junior ranks difficult, it also helped to delay the process of adjusting party strategy to a world of full employment and clamouring consumerism. What was worse, the two leading representaives of the younger generation, Bevan and Gaitskell, had split the party before the debate about future priorities had really got under way. Taken together, these three factors – the need to attract more cross-class support, the void at the heart of Labour policy by 1951 and the disastrous Bevan Gaitskell dispute – clouded the legacy of Labour's 'finest hour'. As David Howell reflects, this period 'might have been the party's heroic age, but like many feats of heroism it had a devastating effect on the hero'.[60]

2
YEARS OF OPPOSITION, 1951–64

I

'After 1951', according to James Hinton, 'the labour movement entered into a long drawn out and, as yet, unresolved crisis'.[1] Historians and political commentators are generally agreed that, after the heady days of the Attlee government, Labour went into prolonged and steep decline. Much of the evidence speaks for itself. The number of Labour voters fell from 14 million in 1951 to 11 million in 1987; the party's trade union base was steadily eroded in the wake of profound changes to the industrial workforce; and individual Labour party membership dropped alarmingly – by at least three quarters from its high point in the early 1950s. In this longer-term framework, the thirteen frustrating years in opposition after 1951 have traditionally been portrayed as marking the origins of Labour's downward slide. The party's poor electoral showing in the 1950s was clearly the result, in part, of factional in-fighting of the sort that had been absent immediately after the war. Labour's reaction to the loss of power in 1951 was to enter into protracted internal disputes: between Bevanite 'fundamentalists' advocating extensions of public ownership and Gaitskellite 'revisionists' seeking to play down nationalisation at the expense of social justice. 'The internal atmosphere of the party during these years',

35

notes David Howell, 'was one of bitterness and intolerance. Party Conferences became theatres in which the representatives of Good and Evil mixed declarations of principle and imputations of base motives to the background of partisan demonstrations from the floor'.[2]

Early explanations of Labour's electoral malaise tended to be a continuation of this power struggle by other means. Left-wing commentators attributed the party's electoral difficulties to the growing ascendancy of revisionist ideas. According to Ralph Miliband, by abandoning a consciously socialist perspective in the early 1950, Labour both betrayed its ideals and alienated its natural supporters.[3] Conversely, revisionists believed that the party was not adapting itself quickly enough to post-war social change. In particular, it was argued that as Conservative governments provided wider home ownership and steady economic growth – thereby allowing greater access to consumer goods such as cars and domestic appliances – so the 'affluent worker' was increasingly aspiring to middle-class habits and abandoning the Labour party.[4] Subsequent research has exposed the inadequacies of these arguments, both in oversimplifying the nature of post-war society and in underrating the residual strength of the Labour vote, which was sufficient to produce a majority government in 1964. Here it will be argued that the long years of opposition should not be interpreted as part of a process of inexorable long-term decline. Rather, as James Cronin has noted, for a generation after 1950 'Britain exhibited a pattern of structural change whose undiluted political effect could well have been to maintain, or possibly to increase, Labour support.' Full employment, increased numbers of women at work, and the proliferation of white-collar jobs – all allowed trade unions, a vital source of Labour strength hitherto, to actually increase their membership.[5] Without doubt, Labour struggled to find ways of appealing to those groups at the heart of social change, such as younger voters, but so too did the Conservatives; such a failing only became of real importance when Labour returned to power and proved incapable of delivering popular, defensible policies. The party's electoral slide, in other words, had as much to with political as social determinants, and only really got under way after 1964, when it missed the opportunity of establishing itself as the natural party of government. Labour's weakness in the 1950s might therefore be accounted for in more straightforward terms. In a period of sustained economic growth, with living standards rising rapidly, there was no compelling incentive to change the government of the day, especially as the opposition seemed more concerned with its own internal differences. In practice, as we shall see, Labour's factional strife often focused on foreign rather than domestic policy. But for ordinary voters, the image was of a party that had traded the unity of the Attlee years for 'civil war' between rival clans. In order to demonstrate how such bitterness developed, and with what consequence, it is first necessary to look at reactions to Labour's electoral defeat in October 1951.

II

'What is really significant', wrote back-bencher and diarist Richard Crossman on the first day of the new parliament, 'is the cheerfulness and morale of the Party, compared with its state of semi-disintegration just before the election'.[6] For several months, Labour MPs were convinced that the new Churchill government would run into difficulties. When their hopes were confounded, the optimism noted by Crossman began to dissipate, and pre-election tensions resurfaced with a vengeance. In March 1952, after a series of acrimonious meetings, a group of 57 MPs defied the party whip by refusing to back an official amendment to the defence estimates. This marked the first major act of public defiance by the Bevanites, a group within the parliamentary party that developed out of the ranks of the Keep Left group of the Attlee years. What made this challenge more significant was that, for the first time in a generation, the left had a leader who could attract support throughout the broader Labour movement. Bevan was credited with both successful ministerial experience and outstanding skills as an orator, and in 1952 he attempted to build on this by publishing his own political creed. *In Place of Fear* argued that in order to challenge the power structures of British society, it was necessary that democratic socialism become something more than a middle way between capitalism and communism. Bevan's work was much criticised for failing to take into account changes since the war, and for proposing remedies that seemed more appropriate to the economic circumstances of the 1930s. Nevertheless, there were signs that the tide was running in his direction. In the localities, individual party membership continued to grow, with many drawn in by Bevan's charisma; the Bevanite journal *Tribune* was successfully relaunched with a rising circulation; and constituency parties fell over each other to hold 'Brains Trusts' question sessions featuring Bevanite speakers such as Crossman and Barbara Castle. At Westminster, Bevan's supporters organised weekly meetings to discuss policy papers, and were often found socialising together; they constituted not so much 'a party within a party', as critics alleged, but rather 'the Smoking Room within the Smoking Room'.[7]

The increasingly high profile of the Bevanites set alarm bells ringing on the Labour right. Attlee's private belief, that Bevan had the necessary qualities for future leadership, was not widely shared by his senior colleagues, many of whom regarded Bevan as an egocentric demagogue. Those prepared to speak out against Bevanite activity, such as Gaitskell and Herbert Morrison, gradually began to enlist the support of concerned elements within the PLP and the trade union hierarchy. A particular scourge of the Bevanites was the leader of the Transport Workers, Arthur Deakin, described by one of his opponents as 'the poor man's Ernest Bevin, with the same tendency to gut reactions, the same ruthlessness in crushing opposition, but without the least scintilla of Bevin's intelligence or skills'.[8] It was Deakin who pressed for tough disciplinary action, including threats of expulsion from the party, after the back-bench revolt over defence in March 1952. The outcome of a protracted inquest into this incident was the reintroduction of Standing Orders, suspended since 1945; henceforth MPs could only receive the whip if they agreed to stand by majority decisions of the parliamentary party. The revival of Standing Orders clearly marked the eclipse of the unity that characterised the immediate post-war years. Attlee himself, while regretting this new departure, believed that he had gone as far as possible in disciplining the rebels without causing an open rupture in party ranks; only if party unity was maintained, he believed, did Labour have any realistic chance of removing Churchill from power. The dispute over defence also convinced Attlee of the need to remain as party leader for the foreseeable future. He calculated that if he stood down, union block votes would ensure the succession of Morrison, whose antagonistic approach to the Bevanites was certain to widen existing divisions.[9] In the event, tensions increased at an alarming rate in spite of Attlee's best efforts to adopt a conciliatory line. Nowhere was this more evident than at the party's annual conference in the autumn of 1952.

'The Morecambe Conference', recalled Attlee-loyalist Douglas Jay, 'was memorable as one of the most unpleasant experiences I ever suffered in the Labour Party. The town was ugly, the hotels forbidding, the weather bad, and the Conference, at its worst, hideous'.[10] Normal courtesies were cast aside as right-wing speakers found themselves booed and jeered from the gallery; one union leader was so provoked that he shouted at delegates 'Shut yer gob'.[11] What was more, the advance of Bevanite ideas within the party was reflected in the passing of motions backing the principle of a free health service and demanding further nationalisation of 'key and major industries'. The most bitter feelings were reserved for the elections to the constituency section of the National Executive Committee (NEC). When the results were announced, two of the party's old guard, Morrison and Hugh Dalton, had been knocked off the Executive by two leading Bevanites, Harold Wilson and Dick Crossman. The Bevanites, who could now claim six out of seven constituency places on the NEC, were not afraid to exult in their triumph. News of Morrison's defeat in particular was greeted with howls of delight on the conference floor, and Harold Wilson was heard to remark that 'Nye's little dog has turned round and bitten Dalton where it hurts'. It was no wonder that many present considered the party conference the worst in Labour's history. Nor was any early improvement likely. To many on the right, Morecambe demonstrated that if Bevanites in the Commons were an irritation, then Bevanism in the country threatened the whole future of the Labour movement. In a hard-hitting speech at Stalybridge the week after the conference, Hugh Gaitskell provoked his opponents by calling for an end to 'mob rule by a group of frustrated journalists'. Hugh Dalton noted in his diary that 'nothing is getting better. More hatred, and more love of hatred, in our Party than I ever remember'.[12]

What then was at stake in this bitter feuding? In part the conflict was a battle for the party leadership. With Attlee likely to retire in the not too distant future, union leaders such as Deakin were determined that he should be replaced by Morrison or, after the Stalybridge speech, by Gaitskell. Equally, the left had its own ambitions. Gaitskell once commented that Bevan 'just wants to lead the Party, and that is all the Bevanites want'; if this was the case, then Bevan sought the leadership through converting the party to his ideas, and not through the type of power brokerage that union leaders could exercise.[13] The implication here was that the clash between left and right was mainly ideological – in Bevan's words, there was a 'basic conflict over party purpose', between fundamentalists and revisionists. But in reality, some important qualifications must be added. In the first place, party disputes in the early 1950s were much less concerned with domestic than with foreign affairs. The principal topics of concern were German rearmament, national service and nuclear weapons. Whereas over twenty back-bench revolts took place on foreign policy and defence, only one was over nationalisation.[14] Secondly, neither side had any coherently formulated ideology to apply to domestic politics. Bevanism focused almost exclusively on demands for nationalisation, while the right had not as yet produced any distinctly revisionist agenda; those younger, middle-class MPs who were floating new ideas tended to be viewed with suspicion by old-style trade unionists.[15] There were, moreover, many shared assumptions between left and right, notably over the achievements of the Attlee government. Contributors to a 1952 collection of *New Fabian Essays*, drawn from all sections of the party, were agreed that – in contrast to 1930s Britain – the power of capitalism could be subordinated and shaped by the political decisions of a democratic state. This collection also indicated, moreover, that there was a sizeable 'centre' element within the party, many of whom believed that internal feuding was a futile distraction. What this really left, at the heart of the bitterness in the early 1950s, were differences of political style and emphasis, compounded by a rapid hardening of individual loyalties. The whole dispute soon became, in the words of Douglas Jay, 'a notable case of what Thucydides, in his account of the civil war in Corfu calls "statis": faction for faction's sake in which the protagonists know which side they are on, but usually cannot remember why it all started'.[16]

In the aftermath of the Morecambe conference, Attlee decided that the time had come to attempt a firm stand. At the first meeting of MPs in the new parliamentary session, he secured agreement by 188 votes to 51 for a resolution banning all unofficial groups within the party. Under protest, the Bevanites had no but option to comply. Thereafter, instead of a forty strong group, Bevanism in the parliamentary party was restricted to a smaller, private lunch discussion group, containing only Bevan's closest followers, such as Michael Foot, Ian Mikardo, Richard Crossman and Harold Wilson. Bevan himself also believed the time had come to mend fences. In the belief that the Morecambe conference had endorsed many of the policy positions favoured by the left, he now put himself forward for shadow cabinet elections as a signal that he was prepared to re-enter the party mainstream. The result was that throughout 1953 and early 1954 an 'armed truce' persisted. Old antagonisms remained beneath the surface and still occasionally flickered into life, most notably over the question of whether Germany should be permitted to develop independent national forces or be contained within a wider western alliance.[17] But on all sides there was a recognition that Churchill's government, enjoying the fruits of economic advance, could only be seriously challenged if Labour displayed unity. Hence the disruptive scenes in Morecambe were not repeated at the Margate conference in 1953. Instead, delegates approved almost unanimously a compromise policy document entitled *Challenge to Britain*, which combined limited promises of nationalisation with a pledge to remove all charges on the National Health Service.

In the spring of 1954, however, the armed truce was superseded by a return to more open warfare. Bevan found it ever more difficult to tolerate being in a minority of one in the shadow cabinet, especially as Conservative popularity made it increasingly unlikely that his self discipline would be rewarded by a return to high office. In a debate on foreign policy, Bevan's frustrations got the better of him when he launched a scathing attack that appeared to contradict most of what Attlee had argued on behalf of the party. After receiving a stern rebuke for what many MPs regarded as megalomania, Bevan announced his resignation from the shadow cabinet. Aside from leading to a formal ruling that in future front-bench speakers should stick to defined subjects, this incident had serious implications for the balance of power within the party. In the first place, the disintegration of the Bevanites was confirmed when the runner-up in shadow cabinet elections, Harold Wilson, decided to take his mentor's place, thus provoking allegations of 'MacDonaldism' from those on the left. In addition, Bevan had seriously undermined any prospect of succeeding Attlee in due course. He had not only alienated mainstream party opinion, but had also disappointed his friends, who recognised that outside the shadow cabinet he had much less authority to promote his ideas. This was confirmed later in the year when he was easily defeated by Hugh Gaitskell for the post of party treasurer. 'Bevan', noted Hugh Dalton in December 1954, 'has been committing slow suicide', and this, combined with the 'melancholy mediocrity of Morrison', made it increasingly likely that Attlee might be succeeded by Gaitskell.[18] 'The trouble with Nye', one of his supporters later concluded, 'was that he wasn't a team player'.[19] He could neither work closely with senior colleagues nor, owing to his conviction that socialism was about instinct rather than strategy, provide the consistent forward planning sought by his allies; in this sense, Bevan himself was not really a Bevanite. As if to underline the point, he launched a further attack on Attlee in a defence debate in March 1955; this led, despite the imminence of a general election, to another bout of wrangling in which Bevan only narrowly escaped expulsion from the party.[20]

The price of Labour's internecine warfare soon became apparent. After Churchill's retirement, his successor Anthony Eden could not resist calling an early election in May 1955. The electoral omens had not looked good for Labour for some time. In 45 contested by-elections since 1951, the Conservatives had not suffered a single defeat; unusually in mid-term, several contests had actually seen a swing towards the government. 'I see no reason', lamented Hugh Dalton in private, 'except for crass conservatism, for voting Labour now. The Tories are doing well, Full Employment, Buy What You Like, More for all . . .'[21] In such circumstances, Labour found it difficult to make any distinctive appeal to the electorate. The party's manifesto was essentially a re-working of *Challenge to Britain*, which Bevan had described privately as 'cold porridge stirred through a blanket'. Neither appeals to the memory of the 1945 government nor promises of a few further measures of nationalisation did much to stir voters. Indeed the major problem for Labour was how to inject some life into what Dalton described as the 'most tedious, apathetic, uninteresting and . . . worst organised' of all the elections in which he had fought.[22] In the constituencies, Labour suffered from a serious fall in its number of full-time agents since 1951, and attacks on high prices made little impact on the steady Tory lead in the opinion polls. Even Attlee's request that Eden repudiate his 'dirty' electioneering claim that Labour would bring back rationing failed to instill life into a low-key campaign. When the results were announced, it came as no surprise that the Conservatives became the first government in peacetime for nearly a century to be returned to power with an increased majority. Press commentators were agreed about the causes of this outcome: in addition to Labour's internal feuding, 'a great many working people are "doing nicely, thank you" – and they don't bother to ask why . . .'[23] But it would be misleading to depict the 1955 result as part of an inexorable decline. Both parties recorded lower total votes than in 1951 owing to a fall in turnout, and the Conservatives gained only eleven seats on a small average swing of 1.8 per cent. With Labour still commanding 46.4 per cent of the popular vote, there was no indication that this second successive defeat was irreversible.

III

In the aftermath of election defeat, there was a recognition within Labour ranks of the need for change. Party organisation was compared by Harold Wilson to a 'rusty penny-farthing', and a series of research projects designed to reconsider party policy was soon initiated. The major preoccupation of activists, however, as

LIVERPOOL
JOHN MOORES UNIVERSITY
TRUEMAN STREET LIBRARY
TEL. 051 231 4022/4023

they faced up to the prospect of a lengthy Eden administration, was with the party leadership. It was obvious that Attlee, after twenty years at the helm, would soon retire, and the question of his successor occasioned intense speculation. At the first party meeting after the election, MPs formally approved Attlee's suggestion that he continue in post for the time being. His motives for staying on, instead of retiring immediately, have been variously interpreted. Critics claim that Attlee was determined all along to spite his long-standing rival, Herbert Morrison; hence he clung on until 'Morrison's last hope had vanished'.[24] On the other hand, Attlee believed that his immediate resignation was likely to deepen the divisions between right and left by leaving the way open for open warfare between the supporters of Morrison and Bevan. Whatever his motives, the practical effect of Attlee's decision was to greatly enhance the prospects of a third contender for the leadership, Hugh Gaitskell. Aside from a forceful conference performance, revealing a passion for social justice hitherto hidden from many party members, Gaitskell's standing was further enhanced by 'Operation Avalanche' – the effort of his old ally Hugh Dalton to dislodge ageing members of the shadow cabinet, nine of whom were over 65. By encouraging others to follow his lead in making way for younger candidates, Dalton helped to encourage the view that Morrison's age made him an unsuitable leader. With Bevan's record of rebellion undermining his prospects, Dalton was confident that 'H.G. has the Leadership in the Bag'.[25] This was borne out when Attlee finally resigned in December 1955. In the ballot among back-benchers that followed, Gaitskell comfortably defeated Bevan, leaving Morrison humiliated in third place.[26]

There were several factors that explained the ease of Gaitskell's succession. As one of his closest associates was later to observe:

It had become clear to those who a feared a resumption of Bevan's excesses that a vote for Gaitskell was now the best way of holding the Party together. Though still under fifty, Gaitskell shared with Stafford Cripps one rare quality which was immensely valued by the solid core of Labour MPs. By calculated lucidity and unadorned rational argument, he in the end produced a more *emotional* conviction than rhetoric could achieve. Bevan's most splendid speeches entertained, impressed, even enthused. . . . But Gaitskell's *persuaded*; and left conviction where there had previously been doubt.[27]

The new leader was not without his critics. In personal terms, even his close allies admitted to 'a streak of intolerance in Gaitskell's nature; he tended to believe that no one could disagree with him unless they were either knaves or fools'.[28] And to many Bevanites, of course, it was not easy to forgive Gaitskell's close ties with the party's right-wing since 1951. The claim that Gaitskell was insufficiently radical to head the Labour party – which Attlee once said should always be led from left-of centre – was one that was to resurface at various times for years to come. So too were the accusations that he relied too heavily on a narrow clique of friends known as the 'Hampstead set', who like himself tended to be middle-class and Oxford-educated. In these circumstances, it was to Gaitskell's credit that he was able to so rapidly establish himself as party leader. He first managed to exploit the mood for a fresh start by offering past antagonists such as Bevan and Harold Wilson important positions in the new shadow cabinet. Within a year, Gaitskell was also able to demonstrate his potential as a national leader during the Suez crisis. By speaking out so powerfully against the Anglo-French attack on the Egyptians, emphasising the theme of 'law not war', Gaitskell both carried with him the support of the whole Labour movement and played a part in helping to bring down Anthony Eden after the suspension of the Suez operation.[29]

Gaitskell's leadership also meant fresh thinking about the party's domestic agenda. After the 1955 defeat, the NEC identified several areas of investigation, with the aim of revising policy in order to take account of recent social changes. Under Gaitskell's guidance, this process resulted in what became known as Labour's 'revisionist' programme. In place of the old style corporate socialism that had characterised the Attlee generation, the party was gradually moving towards an ideology that stressed the need to achieve greater social equality. Revisionism not only found expression in policy committees; in terms of the intellectual argument, Gaitskell's case was greatly strengthened by the publication in 1956 of Anthony Crosland's work, *The Future of*

Socialism. Crosland, an Oxford-trained economist and a close friend of Gaitskell, argued that one of the main inspirations of British socialism – antagonism towards the evils created by capitalism – was becoming outdated. Now that post-war economic management was capable of delivering much wider prosperity than ever before, attention should be focused more on the ethical tradition in socialist thinking, especially the principle of equality. In order to progress towards equality, Crosland argued, Labour had to draw up a list of new priorities: these included comprehensive schools for all children, the redistribution of wealth via the taxation system, and the utilisation of public expenditure to remedy social injustices in areas such as housing and health. Crosland also believed that socialism could only be relevant to everyday lives if it lost its association with state-directed puritanism of the Cripps variety. 'Total abstinence and a good filing system are not', he claimed, the right sign-posts to the socialist Utopia: or at least, if they are, some of us will fall by the wayside'.[30] The Labour left were outraged by Crosland's belief that nationalisation should henceforth play only a minor role in socialist advance, but for many party activists the synthesising brilliance of *The Future of Socialism* was to make it a vital reference point for a generation to come.

The Bevanite left, by contrast, seemed devoid of new thinking. Bevan himself was scornful of the 'fresh thinkers' who claimed that socialism needed to be reassessed. 'Do we now burn the books?', he questioned. 'Don't we need to bother with William Morris, or Karl Marx, or Keir Hardie?'[31] In spite of differences over public ownership, there were in reality many similarities between the socialism of Bevan and Crosland; where Bevan really parted company was his belief that the revisionists were surrendering to the tide of acquisitive individualism that threatened to destroy communal values. But Bevan himself had never been able to make this concern the basis of a convincing alternative programme, and the retreat of Bevanism within the parliamentary party meant there was only a negligible intellectual challenge to the revisionist case. A small group of back-benchers sought to revive a defunct group known as 'Victory for Socialism', but the few policy pamphlets it produced served mostly to highlight the weakness of the Labour left. Indeed many of the most innovative ideas about socialism in the second half of the 1950s came from outside the party mainstream, from the so-called 'New Left'. This broad movement developed initially amongst Communists disillusioned with Stalinism after the invasion of Hungary in 1956; it was soon joined by those, including academics such as E. P. Thompson and Raymond Williams, who stressed cultural concerns and the need for a more radical conception of politics than now existed within Labour ranks.[32] In the meantime, the champion of the 'old left' was making his peace with the party leader. Bevan recognised, however reluctantly, that Gaitskell's victory in the leadership contest decisively ended the power struggle within the party. After years of frustration on party committees that inevitably reflected the organisational strength of the right, Bevan came to the view that he must henceforth play the role of loyal lieutenant, especially after he was asked to act as shadow Foreign Secretary. The party's future prospects were also an important consideration. Eden's failings as Prime Minister, even before the Suez fiasco, persuaded Bevan like others that Labour had a real prospect of returning to power. While factional differences might smoulder beneath the surface, it was agreed on all sides that there must be no return to the open warfare of the early 1950s.

The new marriage of convenience between Gaitskell and Bevan certainly allowed the party to develop a more coherent pro-gramme. This was seen most dramatically in the case of defence policy. In a famous speech at the annual conference in 1957, Bevan alienated many of his closest followers by declaring that Britain should not unilaterally abandon nuclear weapons. For several years, Bevan had spoken with great passion about the horrors of atomic warfare, and was identified as the natural leader of the unilateralist left within the party. But, as John Campbell notes, Bevan had never opposed the Attlee government's decision to manufacture the bomb, and in many respects he shared the multilateral orthodoxy of the party leadership.[33] After much agonising, Bevan decided to speak at the Brighton conference in favour of an NEC motion which committed a future Labour government to oppose testing, but to halt production of nuclear weapons only if other powers agreed likewise. To endorse the unilateralist alternative, he claimed after being heckled from the floor of the conference, would be to send a British Foreign Secretary 'naked into the conference chamber', which represented not statesmanship but an 'emotional spasm'. Bevan's robust language ensured the defeat of the unilateralist resolution by an overwhelming majority, though it cost him dear in terms of personal friendships; the spectacle of witnessing 'Bevan into Bevin', as the *Daily Telegraph* put it, was something close friends such as Michael Foot could never forgive.[34] His speech highlighted the extent to which Bevan had tied himself to Gaitskell's leadership, and confirmed that Bevanism as a serious force within the parliamentary party was now a thing of the past. It was no coincidence that the forces built up by Bevan in the constituencies and the trade unions now began to channel their energies in new, extraparliamentary directions, most notably into the newly-formed Campaign for Nuclear Disarmament (CND). At the annual conference in 1958, the party's commitment to NATO and to multilateralism was again endorsed, though there was increasing concern about growing support for a more militant position.

Although overshadowed by the drama of the defence debate, the Brighton conference of 1957 also demonstrated the eclipse of the left on domestic policy. With sullen acquiescence from Bevan, the policy sub-committee on public ownership set up by Gaitskell produced a document entitled *Industry and Society*, which committed a future Labour administration to little more than the renationalisation of steel and road haulage. Beyond this, there were only vague references to reviewing the position of industries alleged to be 'failing the nation', and to the possibility of the state controlling investment in private companies by buying a percentage of shares short of ownership.[35] In spite of the fulminations of *Tribune*, this position was overwhelmingly backed by delegates in Brighton, and Gaitskell was credited with a triumph which avoided the need to make any potentially damaging commitments in the run up to a general election. Bevan's behaviour at Brighton was conditioned, at least in part, by the widespread belief that Labour was once again a serious contender for power, and that he would be in a position before long to seriously attempt the task of nuclear disarmament. In the aftermath of Suez, the party maintained a clear lead in the opinion polls throughout 1957. Unlike the early

1950s, Labour could also take comfort from a string of promising by-election results, culminating in the capture of Rochdale and Glasgow Kelvingrove from the Conservatives early in 1958. But belief in certain victory was gradually eroded. Eden's successor as Prime Minister, Harold Macmillan, was soon making capital out of his claim that the nation had 'never had it so good', and within months the government's popularity was restored. By-elections in the first half of 1959 showed virtually no swing towards Labour, and opinion polls in the run up to the election in October 1959 suggested a clear if modest Conservative lead.[36]

Labour went into the election in much better shape than in 1955. There was little evidence of past policy differences. Whatever their reservations in private, the former Bevanites gave full public backing to a manifesto that focused on social justice and played down nationalisation. More so than in 1955, the party also had a leader capable, at least at the outset, of forcing the campaign pace. Ironically, it was Gaitskell himself who made a serious blunder by claiming that Labour's improved social provision would not require increases in income tax. While the effect on voters of a single pledge can easily be exaggerated, this incident did appear to mark a turning point. Thereafter Tory ministers relentlessly made the claim that Labour was cynically bidding for votes with a series of unattainable promises.[37] The outcome was a third successive Conservative victory. On an average swing towards the government of 1.1 per cent, the number of Labour voters fell again and Macmillan was able to increase his overall majority to 100 parliamentary seats. The regional pattern of results indicated that wider prosperity was a key determinant in voting behaviour. Most of Labour's losses were concentrated in London and the West Midlands, areas that had prospered in economic terms during the 1950s, whereas two regions that experienced rising unemployment – Scotland and Lancashire – went against the national trend by recording a small swing to Labour. In many ways this was a more crushing defeat for Labour than 1955. It was no longer possible to blame factional in-fighting, and some commentators were quick to draw the conclusion that the Labour party looked obsolete in the face of rising living standards. There was, however, some reason to remain sceptical about the notion of an eroding Labour vote. The party may not have fared well with voters under thirty – those too young to remember 'the hungry thirties' – but its appeal in industrialised communities still enabled it to retain nearly 44 per cent of the total vote.[38] In reality, any opposition would have found it difficult to dent the popularity of a government that delivered stable prices and steady growth; Gaitskell defended himself by pointing out that on balance fewer than three voters in every 200 had switched sides. The real question for Labour was to decide in which direction it should now move: should more full-blooded socialism be given its chance, or was 'the party's weakness that it had not been revisionist enough?'[39]

IV

Inquests into the causes of the 1959 defeat came to widely differing conclusions. Douglas Jay, reflecting views he encountered on the doorstep during the election, immediately published a controversial article suggesting if the party was to avoid the charge of exclusive association with a shrinking working class, it might have to consider a change of name.[40] To the left it seemed outrageous that the Gaitskellites, having dictated party policy for several years, should claim that defeat demonstrated the need to move further still to the right. Bevan gave vent to his frustration by publicly claiming that Labour had paid the price for fighting not on a socialist programme, but on 'pre-1914 Liberalism brought up to date'. This set the scene for a renewed period of blood-letting which appeared to confirm the worst fears about Labour's future. Gaitskell himself opened up a fresh area of controversy at the annual conference in November 1959. His own explanation for defeat emphasised long-term social changes, but also argued that votes had been lost because of the party's image – especially its association in the public mind with wholesale nationalisation. In common with many of the leading revisionist intellectuals, Gaitskell had long believed that public ownership was only one of several means by which to achieve socialist ends. As a result, he now took the high risk strategy of proposing that the party should amend Clause Four of its 1918 constitution; this was the clause, reprinted on party membership cards, that stipulated the need to aim for the 'common ownership of the means of production, distribution and exchange'.

For some conference delegates, the leader's suggestion was broadly acceptable; if Labour was ever to recover electorally, then modernisation was unavoidable. But this was far from being a typical reaction. Many party activists, including trade union leaders hitherto loyal to Gaitskell, regarded Clause Four as the cornerstone of their political outlook. In the words of Henry Drucker, Clause Four encapsulated the 'ethos' rather than the 'doctrine' of the party. It convinced party members that, come what may, their socialist commitment was fundamentally sound.[41] Gaitskell's proposal was not designed to rule out any further measures of nationalisation by a future government, but simply to attack such a vital symbol was rather like trying to 'persuade Christian fundamentalists that they need not believe in God'.[42] After several months of heated exchanges, the party leader was forced to back down. By focusing on a symbolic issue – which many moderates thought would not be understood by the general public – Gaitskell had helped to deepen party divisions without furthering the process of policy revision. His own advisers had in fact warned him that he would 'start a battle in the Party that will cause far more trouble than the thing is worth'.[43] As a result, Gaitskell has been much criticised for his poor tactical sense, and for fighting the wrong battle at the wrong time. At the outset, however, he cannot have known that his former union allies would desert him, and Gaitskell himself was convinced that it was not the wrong battle to be fighting. If, as he believed, Labour's real problem was not its policies but its image, then it was only by openly demonstrating its willingness to adapt that the party would attract sufficient new voters to secure electoral victory.[44] Nevertheless, the very fact of having to back down over the Clause Four controversy had some serious implications. Henceforth Gaitskell had to acknowledge that attachment to his brand of revisionism was not as widespread in the party as he hoped. In the short-term, criticism was such that the leader even faced an open challenge to his own position.

Unease about the leadership in 1960 crystallised in particular around another high profile issue – that of defence. With its well publicised annual marches from Aldermaston to London, CND was attracting increasing support for the unilateralist cause, not least amongst a minority of Labour MPs. The main challenge to the party's official multilateral policy, however, came from the trade unions. Unlike Attlee, Gaitskell could no longer rely on the backing of the old pro-right triumvirate of transport workers, miners and municipal workers. In particular, Deakin's successor as leader of the Transport Workers' Union, Frank Cousins, was sympathetic to a range of left-wing policy positions, including unilateralism. By aligning supportive elements at the 1960 conference in Scarborough, Cousins was able to use union block votes to ensure the passage of two unilateralist resolutions and the defeat of the leadership's official statement on defence. Gaitskell immediately let it be known that he would not accept the view of conference, in theory the supreme policy-making authority. He argued that a unilateralist position was intellectually disreputable and electorally disastrous, and he pledged to 'fight and fight and fight again' against the decision. Within a matter of weeks, though, the party leader was fighting for his own position. Ever since the 1959 election, there had been an undercurrent of concern about his leadership: a feeling that Gaitskell spent too much of his time imposing his wishes on reluctant followers and not enough seeking to match Macmillan on the national stage. This view was held particularly by the left, and after the death of Nye Bevan in 1960, many of the former Bevanites were prepared to back Harold Wilson in a leadership challenge. Wilson stood not on the basis of support for unilateralism, but rather as a 'unity' candidate, opposed to what was said to be Gaitskell's confrontational style of right-wing leadership. In the event, Gaitskell secured a comfortable, if not overwhelming, victory in the PLP ballot; at the same time, Wilson put down a useful marker for the future.[45]

In retrospect, the leadership contest was the start of an impressive fightback by Gaitskell. During the next year, he was not only able to re-establish his personal authority, but also put the party in a position where it was able to benefit from a turnaround in electoral fortunes. 'The crucial task for the next year', advised one of Gaitskell's supporters, 'is to isolate the extreme left and win back or consolidate the left-centre'.[46] This task was greatly assisted by the emergence in 1960 of the Campaign for Democratic Socialism (CDS), an organised pressure group within the party that sought to disseminate revisionist ideas and to promote revisionists to key positions of power. The new grouping was dominated by 'Hampstead set' Gaitskellites, though it came to have support from about 45 MPs; it also established a youth section and sought to influence local parties and trade unions, though with varying degrees of success on different issues.[47] The most potent symbol of Gaitskell's fightback in 1961, the reversal of conference approval for unilateralism, was only marginally influenced by CDS pressure. Rather some of the major unions, such as those representing the railwaymen and the engineers, decided to endorse a multilateral defence policy in the interests of party unity. The same desire for pulling together could be seen in the support given to a new domestic programme, drawing inspiration from a policy document entitled *Signposts for the Sixties*. This aimed at reconciling different opinions within the party by calling for both social egalitarianism and planning to secure a higher economic growth rate.[48] By securing backing for both his foreign and domestic policies at the 1961 conference, Gaitskell could be satisfied that his authority had been reaffirmed.

There was, moreover, a growing belief by the beginning of 1962 that Gaitskell could well become the next Prime Minister. After the optimism that surrounded the Conservative election victory in 1959, Macmillan's government had been beset by chronic economic difficulties. In particular, the need to impose a 'pay pause' on publicly paid employees was sufficient to push Labour ahead in opinion polls during 1961. By-election results also indicated a government on the run. Although the Liberal party made the headlines with a famous by-election victory at Orpington in 1962, Labour was also making headway; its success at Middlesbrough West was the party's first gain since the general election. Nor was Labour much damaged in the eyes of the electorate by differences of opinion over the major question of foreign policy in the early 1960s – that of whether Britain should join the Common Market. Many on the revisionist wing of the party shared the government's view that British economic interests could only be secured in the long-term by closer integration with continental Europe. But this view was far from universal in Labour ranks. Those on the left saw the Common Market as a suspect capitalist enterprise, while many others disputed the likely economic benefits of membership, and were worried about the possible undermining of national sovereignty. Gaitskell's attitude was influenced by his belief that British membership would irrevocably undermine traditional ties with the Commonwealth and North America. As a result, he made an impassioned speech at the 1962 conference, citing 'a thousand years of history' as a basis for standing aside from Europe.[49] By siding for the first time with mainstream party opinion against his own more natural supporters, Gaitskell managed to avoid any fresh divisions that might jeopardise Labour's electoral prospects. He was not, however, to be the beneficiary of the party's improving fortunes. After a brief illness, Gaitskell died, at the age of fifty-six, from a rare disease early in 1963.

His successor was Harold Wilson. In a hastily convened and entirely unexpected leadership contest, Wilson won sufficient support from the centre-left of the parliamentary party to defeat two candidates of the right, James Callaghan and George Brown. In spite of his background as a Bevanite who had resigned over health service charges in 1951, Wilson essentially belonged to the moderate centre of the PLP, and presented himself as the candidate of reconciliation. He believed, like Attlee, that Labour was best led by maintaining unity between the different wings of the party; in other words, that he should not follow Gaitskell's more abrasive style.[50] Consequently, as he settled down into the leadership, Wilson made sure that his shadow cabinet represented all shades of party opinion. In policy terms, he tended to play down both the revisionist emphasis on achieving social equality and the left-wing case for extending public ownership. Instead he brought to the fore a theme implicit in *Signposts for the Sixties* – namely that socialism was about science. His central argument was that in order to avoid the 'stop-go' economics of the Conservative government, Labour should champion a new managerial revolution. As the party of professional managers, scientists, technicians and skilled workers, Wilson believed, Labour would stand for modernisation, in stark contrast to the Conservatives under their new leader in

1963, the Scottish aristocrat Sir Alec Douglas-Home. 'With Wilson', notes Kenneth Morgan, 'a folksy northener full of reminiscences of Herbert Chapman's Huddersfield Town in the 1920s, ranged against the aristocratic languour of Douglas-Home, the contrast between a down-to-earth modernizing Labour Party and grouse-moor Tory Party of the old school was set out in personal terms'.[51] Nowhere was this more apparent than at the annual conference in October 1963; compared with the last time the party met in Scarborough, this was a 'positive love-feast'.[52] Wilson used the occasion to enthuse delegates, and the wider public audience, about the idea of harnessing the 'white heat' of the technological revolution. There were clearly difficulties inherent in this approach, not least what would happen if technical change did not deliver a high-growth economy. But for the time being Wilson, with his familiar pipe and Gannex macintosh, carried all before him. The party had found both a fresh, confident leader and an agreed political rallying cry, and when Douglas-Home finally called an election in October 1964, there was a confident belief that Labour would at last be returned to power.

The election turned out to be a close run thing. Labour's manifesto built upon the policy-making process of recent years by emphasising the need for growth, innovation and efficiency, and in a series of well publicised speeches Wilson emphasised his commitment to 'a just society, to a dynamic, expanding, confident, and, above all, purposive new Britain'.[53] Labour was generally credited with the better campaign. Whereas Douglas Home appeared ill at ease on television, Wilson exuded confidence. His only moment of defensiveness – as Tory ministers attacked him for implying that strikes might be fomented at election time in the Conservative interest – soon passed as the chairman of a particular company cited publicly referred to his workers as 'poor dears . . . with a pretty poor level of intelligence'. Nevertheless, when the results were announced, it became clear that Douglas-Home had recovered some of the ground lost by the Conservatives in the dark days of 1962–63. On an average swing of 2.9 per cent, Labour managed to win an overall majority of just four parliamentary seats, making ground particularly in the north west and in Scotland. Clearly there was just cause for celebration among

Labour supporters as Harold Wilson took up residence in Downing Street. The party had confounded those sceptics who doubted its future, and had wiped out the losses of three previous elections at a stroke; indeed this was the first outright victory for a 'party of the left' in peacetime since 1906. But there were also good reasons for not reading too much into the result. In the first place, Labour's share of the total vote had barely risen from 1959; 44.1 per cent was the lowest share of any majority government for forty years. What ultimately explained the Labour victory was a rise in Liberal support and a steep fall in the Conservative vote. In addition, certain regions of the country – for example the West Midlands, where Labour suffered from accusations of being 'soft' on immigration – had remained strikingly loyal to the Tory cause. If Labour was to safeguard its tentative hold on office and not waste its new opportunity, Wilson still needed to appeal to many more voters; he needed to prove that Labour was now 'the natural party of government'.

V

The election victory of 1964 was difficult to square with contemporary assessments of 'Labour decline'. Notions of 'betrayal' leading to voter apathy had not been borne out. There had been no echo of the 1945 manifesto, with its ringing declaration that 'we are a Socialist Party, and proud of it', but this had not prevented Labour returning to power. Equally, the idea that the aspiring, 'affluent worker' would inevitably turn to the Conservatives as material conditions improved had taken a hard knock. Indeed detailed research into the relationship between social class and voting behaviour, carried out in the early 1960s, found little to support the so-called 'embourgeoisement' thesis. Among workers in Luton, for example, rapidly rising prosperity had not seriously eroded class concerns. Manual workers overwhelmingly saw themselves as working class, and they seldom mixed with white-collar employees, who more openly aspired to middle-class status. In political terms, support for Labour was becoming less instinctive and more conditional, dependent on whether the party might deliver on its stated promises. But most workers still saw Labour as 'our party'; the share of the vote going to Labour had fallen only marginally since 1951.[54] Recent studies have found a similar pattern elsewhere in the country. A growing concern with home-centred life-styles had not yet eroded varied local networks of collective institutions, such as working men's clubs, though Labour's task was becoming more difficult as memories of the war and reconstruction faded.[55] It was also the case that interest in politics generally was diminishing in a more leisure orientated society; individual membership of the Labour party fell from its peak of just over a million in 1952 to 830,000 in 1964. But all the sound and fury of internal divisions in the 1950s had not undermined confidence about the future throughout the move-ment. With electoral backing, and secure in the knowledge that the alliance between the PLP, constituency activists and trade unionists remained firm, Harold Wilson had every reason to hope that the next Labour administration would prove as successful as the last.

There were nevertheless underlying difficulties for Labour that the 1964 result served to obscure, two of them in particular likely to come to the fore if for any reason Wilson's government failed to satisfy expectations. In the first place, the party may have retained the loyalty of many of its traditional supporters, but it had not seriously considered future strategies for coping with social change. Discussion of the affluent society usually focused on the problems it created rather than the opportunities it might afford. As a result, the chance to build up new loyalties among the rapidly expanding ranks of service-sector workers, especially women, was largely spurned.[56] Secondly, in spite of outward appearances, the long civil war of the 1950s had not been satisfactorily resolved in the minds of many Labour activists. Bevanite fundamentalism had obviously failed to make any decisive breakthrough and had been branded by its opponents as irrelevant to modern needs. As one Tory MP wrote shortly after the death of Bevan: 'In the coalfield from which he came, Marx and Engels have been supplanted by Marks and Spencer; and the sound of class war is drowned by the hum of the spin dryer.'[57] But in view of the Gaitskellite domination of party institutions from 1955 onwards, the real surprise was that revisionism was not able to triumph more completely. The reason for this was that old-style fundamentalist socialism may have been down, but it was not out. As the Clause Four controversy vividly illustrated, there remained deep-seated attachment throughout the party to traditional symbols and rhetoric. The uneasy compromise that followed, which partly rehabilitated public ownership, meant that Labour could never follow the example of its German counterpart in fully embracing a 'competitive society'. It thus remained unclear which of the party's main traditions would ultimately prevail, especially as Harold Wilson used the theme of scientific revolution as a means of binding together his forces while avoiding the hard question: was Labour now a party of socialism or social democracy?[58]

This raises, finally, the issue of the Labour leadership in the early 1960s. Gaitskell's adherents have insisted that, but for his untimely death, he would have made an excellent Prime Minister, capable of showing a 'sureness of purpose' that had not been seen since the days of the 1945 government.[59] On the other hand, as we have seen, Gaitskell in power would still have been faced with those who resented efforts to mould the party in his own image; it was not long after his death that Gaitskell was being openly attacked for his 'uninventive mind' and his 'succession of political blunders'.[60] Wilson's accession to the leadership brought with it a rather different set of possibilities and potential problems. From the outset, he demonstrated both adeptness as a party manager and an ability to appeal to a wider, public audience. But these qualities alone did not mean that he was necessarily more suited to the demands of the premiership. With hindsight, it can be seen that Labour's 1964 election victory was won at the cost of greatly raising expectations. By linking socialism with science, Wilson could persuasively claim to have modernised the party in a matter of months, where Gaitskell had failed over years. 'With one bound Jack was free – or so . . . it was possible to believe'.[61] And yet in many respects Labour seemed ill-equipped to deliver a high-growth, diversified economy, having thought little for example about the reaction of trade unionists to the rapidly changing working patterns that inevitably accompanied technological change. Similarly, there were dangers in making bold promises to the electorate. At the same time as maintaining Britain's various global commitments, Wilson pledged that a new Labour government would reverse the stagnation of the Tory years by using 'socialist planning' to produce a dynamic, classless society; a society in which the elimination of poverty and the creation of genuine equality of opportunity would become the 'immediate targets of political action', rather than vague ideals. Some seasoned political observers doubted whether the steely commitment to national regeneration shown by Attlee's generation could be emulated by Harold Wilson, a leader who had unsettled colleagues during the 1964 election campaign by insisting that strategy was best decided not with forward planning but on a day to day basis. The wisdom of raising hopes that there could be some sort of re-run of 1945 was about to be put to the test.

3

THE WILSON GOVERNMENTS, 1964–70

I

Immediately after Harold Wilson informed cabinet colleagues of his intention to retire as Prime Minister in 1976, he was taken aside and told by Jim Callaghan: 'Harold, I believe history will treat you more kindly than your contemporaries.'[1] As yet, there have been few signs that this prophecy will be borne out. In particular, the historical reputation of Wilson's 1964 government, which was re-elected with a larger majority in 1966, remains extremely low. As Kenneth Morgan has observed, paraphrasing Bernard Shaw, 'it has no friends and even its enemies don't like it'.[2] For many of those Labour activists who placed their faith in Wilson's optimistic promises of a brave new world, this was to be an era of bitter disillusionment – a period which at home brought not economic modernisation but a lower growth rate than the Tory 'wasted years', and which abroad saw British backing for unpopular American involvement in Vietnam. Wilson's record looks especially threadbare when set against the achievements of the Attlee years:

The Government began with a vague optimism unsupported by a clear substantive programme. There could be no sharper contrast with 1945. The contrast continued through the next six years. The earlier experience had been the heroic ... climateric of British social democracy. The later experience witnessed its decline into mere rhetoric, worldly pragmatism and an open worship of the most traditional symbols of British society. Despite its problems, the Attlee Government had maintained some sense of identity with its working class base and a feeling that great changes were being enacted. After 1964 there were no equivalents.[3]

Some recent accounts have suggested the need to at least partly qualify criticism of Wilson's premiership. There were undoubtedly redeeming features. The government did achieve some of its objectives, such as the introduction of comprehensive secondary education and modest redistribution of wealth; and it could also claim to have played a part in liberalising the law on a variety of issues ranging from equal pay for women to homosexuality.[4] In addition, it must be recognised that Labour came to power in extremely difficult circumstances, inheriting an economy in which the problems of low investment and declining competitiveness were becoming ever more apparent. Those who point the finger of blame at Harold Wilson must, as David Marquand has argued, be more precise about what were avoidable failures and what were the 'the products of structural factors or unforeseeable contingencies beyond the control of any government'.[5] In reviewing the record of the Wilson years, this chapter will attempt to demonstrate the importance of distinguishing between national and party consid- erations. Needless to say, it would be inappropriate to blame an individual Prime Minister for failing to arrest Britain's deep-seated 'economic decline', however much particular policy decisions might be criticised. But Wilson, with all the power at his disposal, can be held to account for the disastrous legacy which this period left for the Labour party. His shortcomings helped to produce a resurgence of damaging internal squabbles, not to mention the abandonment of the party by many local activists and the alienation of large numbers of Labour's traditional supporters. What was remarkable about these developments – which with hindsight marked a decline in Labour's fortunes more serious than anything experienced in the 1950s – was the speed at which the rot set in after 1966. When he came to power, Harold Wilson looked set fair to become one of the most dynamic of Britain's twentieth-century premiers, and for the next eighteen months there were few signs of the disintegration that was to follow.

II

Wilson modelled himself on Clem Attlee. From the moment he entered Downing Street in 1964, the new Prime Minister sought to present himself as a detached but dignified leader, ideally suited to reconciling different viewpoints within the party.[6] An early example came with the formation of Wilson's cabinet, which was careful to balance representatives of both the right and left traditions. Most of the senior positions went to former Gaitskellites, such as Jim Callaghan – who became Chancellor of the Exchequer – and George Brown, who headed the newly-formed Department of Economic Affairs (DEA). But the claims of former Bevanites were also recognised, for example by the appointments of Barbara Castle and Frank Cousins, the latter brought in from the union movement to head another forward-looking creation, the Ministry of Technology. This balancing act was not, however, made from the same position of strength as Attlee enjoyed in 1945. From the outset, there was nobody in Wilson's team to take on the role formerly played by Ernest Bevin, that of a powerful ally who could help to dominate cabinet proceedings. Indeed, Wilson was well aware that most of his colleagues had not supported him in the leadership contest of 1963, and it was no coincidence that his two rivals at that time, Callaghan and Brown, were given posts which led to much of their energy being absorbed in inter-departmental rivalry.[7] In time it also became evident that Wilson, coming from a provincial lower-middle class background, lacked Attlee's great inner confidence. His isolation from senior colleagues led to a growing reliance on a 'kitchen cabinet' of personal advisers, notably his political secretary Marcia Williams, whose influence came to be deeply resented.[8] But in the short-term, there were strong incentives to maintain unity. The narrowness of Labour's election victory dictated an overriding objective: the need for the government to remain in power long enough to be able to fight another contest on its own terms. In order to succeed in this, Wilson had to demonstrate the type of high-powered leadership promised in opposition, especially in his handling of economic policy.

Labour inherited an appalling economic legacy in 1964. In seeking to engineer a pre-election boom, the Conservatives had allowed imports to far outstrip any rise in export trade, with the result that Wilson was greeted by officials with the news that Britain now had a record balance-of-payments deficit. Within days, the Prime Minister – in consultation with Callaghan and Brown – had ruled out one possible remedy: a devaluation of sterling aimed at restoring the competitivenss of British goods abroad. This decision has been much criticised subsequently. Some Labour ministers did actually argue in 1964 for devaluation, which was eventually forced on Wilson three years later when much of the government's economic credibility had been undermined.[9] But at the time there were compelling arguments against tampering with the exhange rate. 'Devaluation would sweep us away', the Prime Minister told one colleague, implying that Labour would be hard put to win a second election if it was branded as the party that admitted to the weakness of Britain's currency. In economic terms, ministers also believed that sterling's over-valuation could be corrected by other means, such as increased productivity and new agreements between employers and unions to ensure an effective prices and incomes policy.[10] These aims were at the heart of the 'National Plan' announced by the DEA in 1965, which promised to build on the co-operation of all sides of industry to produce a 25 per cent growth in national output. Behind the scences, the work of the DEA was already hamstrung by a lack of clearly defined executive powers, and by friction with the Treasury as the main formulator of economic policy.[11] But for the time being, Brown's department could be presented to the public as the driving force of a strategy that was already delivering results. By the end of 1965, Wilson could claim that pensions had been raised, in spite of hostility from those hoping to see welfare reform shelved, and also that an export drive had helped to reduce the balance-of-payments deficit. 'To achieve this, and hold unemployment below 2 per cent at the same

.', recalls one minister, 'gave one even then some sober satisfaction; but by the standards of the 1970s it was almost miraculous'.[12]

The government's commitment to defend sterling was also inextricably linked with its perception of British influence overseas. Shortly after coming to power, Wilson proclaimed his belief in the need to maintain Britain's global commitments. 'We are', he argued, 'a world power and world influence or we are nothing'.[13] And yet, in practice, the Prime Minister recognised – like his post-war predecessors – that in order to preserve the remnants of world power, there was no option but to rely on the Atlantic Alliance. During 1965 Wilson went so far as to negotiate a secret deal with the USA: any devaluation of sterling, which the Americans feared would disrupt their own trade, was ruled out in return for lavish support on the foreign exhanges.[14] The British government also agreed to maintain, at enormous cost, its military bases east of Suez – a crucial concern for President Johnson as the Americans became ever more embroiled in Vietnam. Wilson's attempt to act as a mediator in the Vietnamese conflict came to nothing, and by the time of Labour's annual conference in 1965 disquiet with this aspect of foreign policy was growing apace, constrained only by the prospect of a general election. The importance of the American connection demonstrated itself in numerous ways. A small group of senior ministers, for example, had already decided to continue purchasing Polaris nuclear weapons; a secret decision that ran counter to the spirit if not the letter of Labour's 1964 manifesto. In Rhodesia, the Prime Minister reacted to a unilateral declaration of independence from British control by ruling out military intervention, opting instead for the imposition of economic sanctions. Although he confidently asserted that this would bring down the 'illegal' white regime, Wilson subsequently put no pressure on the USA to comply with sanctions, thus effectively ensuring that the Rhodesian problem would rumble on unresolved.[15]

Any ambiguities in the government's record did not appear to damage the Prime Minister's standing in public eyes. Labour's slim majority was endangered when its attempt to secure a 'safe' seat for the Foreign Secretary, Patrick Gordon-Walker, backfired as the

Conservatives swept to victory in the Leyton by-election of January 1965. Gordon-Walker, defeated in the 1964 election after an overtly racist campaign by his Tory opponent at Smethwick, was duly forced to resign from high office. Over the summer the opposition briefly edged ahead in the opinion polls: this stemmed from a combination of expenditure cutbacks and the election of a new Conservative leader, Edward Heath, in place of Douglas-Home. But in many respects Wilson was at his best in 1965. He relished the challenge of surviving on a day-to-day basis, and his confident manner at the despatch box was often favourably contrasted with Heath's more dogged approach. For the nation at large, Wilson was still a fresh, populist figure, a man who got things done. In addition to the abolition of prescription charges and greater security of tenure in rented housing, he could claim that more genuine opportunities in education were opening up now that local authorities were being urged to introduce comprehensive schools.[16] By the end of 1965, Wilson's personal appeal, combined with a defensible economic record, had put the government back on course. Wilson always made much of the constraints imposed by a small parliamentary majority, and his determination to seek a fresh mandate was reinforced by the Hull North by-election early in 1966. Tory hopes of repeating their success at Leyton were confounded when the Labour candidate held the seat with the largest pro-government swing at a by-election for more than a decade.[17] Within weeks, the Prime Minister had called another election.

The campaign that followed rarely flickered into life. In part this reflected voter fatigue at the prospect of a second contest within two years; but equally important was the general agreement about the likely outcome. Labour now held all the best cards. As in the 1964 campaign, Wilson dominated proceedings, inspiring the party faithful and using his 'family doctor' image to reassure voters in a series of masterful television performances. Aside from outstripping Heath in terms of personal popularity, the Prime Minister was on strong ground in discussing policy. He could point to low unemployment and a reduced balance-of-payments deficits as signs of economic progress; all that was required to complete the job was a reasonable working majority and a full parliamentary

... Difficulties since coming to power could still plausibly be blamed on the Conservatives, and Heath's espousal of new economic remedies, such as trade union reform, was rebutted with requests to know why such policies had not been tried in thirteen years of Tory rule.[18] It therefore came as no great surprise when Labour won an overall majority of 96 parliamentary seats: an outcome which by any reckoning makes it difficult to sustain the idea of inevitable Labour decline. March 1966 was the first occasion in the twentieth century when an incumbent Prime Minister had secured a second electoral victory with an increased majority. It also demonstrated beyond doubt that Labour could win in peacetime, and that the 1945 landslide had not been a one-off success caused by the exceptional circumstances of war.

Wilson's triumph was not as comprehensive as Attlee's victory, though it was distinctive in several ways. The margin between the two parties in their share of the vote (48 per cent to 42 per cent) was wider than at any election since the war. And the uniformity of the swing across the country allowed Labour to gain seats that had not been captured even in 1945. These included the likes of Aberdeen South in Scotland, Lancaster and Middleton in northern England and Oxford, Hampstead and Exeter in the south. Wilson's success must of course be seen in part as a vote of no confidence in the Conservatives, whose vote fell by half a million on a reduced turnout. Voter reaction in 1966 indicated that the Tories were still suffering from the image forged in the dying days of Macmillan's regime, of a party out of touch and dominated by an old fashioned, aristocratic elite.[19] But this only underlined Wilson's success in completing a role reversal. In contrast to the 1950s, it was Labour that now presented itself as a modernising, 'classless' party, whereas the Conservatives were tarred with the brush of being a spent force. If nothing else, the 1966 result had confounded those who doubted in 1959 whether Labour could ever win again. Here was an ideal bridgehead from which to build for the future. Looking back on the euphoria in party ranks that accompanied the election result, one of the Prime Minister's associates said that Labour could now indisputably make itself the party of economic efficiency and social justice. 'Surely now', he believed, 'Harold Wilson, having served his apprenticeship in the highest office of

State, would fulfil . . . the personal hope of millions that he would transcend in achievement the fine work of Clement Attlee'.[20]

III

A more prophetic contemporary note was struck by Tony Benn, an aspiring young minister who wrote in his diary that since Wilson's 'success in the eyes of the public . . . is greater than is perhaps justified by his real achievements, so, when the moment comes for mistakes and failures, these too may be made to seem far greater than they are'.[21] The Prime Minister was certainly cut down to size in the eighteen months after the election. Within weeks, the first dark cloud appeared on the horizon in the form a seamen's strike. Ministers opposed union demands for a six per cent pay rise on the grounds that it would lead to a flood of higher claims. Wilson, to the dismay of many MPs, angrily blamed the stoppage on Communist agitation, and by the time the seamen returned to work in the summer the government had suffered a double blow. With the London docks paralysed, the recovery in the balance-of-payments – patiently built up since 1964 – was severely disrupted. In addition, the strike undermined Labour's claim that an incomes policy would help to transform the British economy. For several months past wage settlements had been running well ahead of inflation, and when moves were made to initiate statutory delays in wage rises, union leaders responded with the claim that workers were being the made the scapegoats for the government's own failings. In July Frank Cousins resigned from the Ministry of Technology, complaining that industrialists were not being asked to make equivalent sacrifices. 'In a free for all', Cousins asserted on behalf of the unions, 'we must be part of the all'.[22] Worse still, the atmosphere of industrial unease confirmed the suspicions of foreign bankers about Labour's handling of the economy. Sterling again came under pressure, falling to its lowest level for twenty months, and publication of figures for gold losses turned nervousness into panic. The government's honeymoon had been remarkably short-lived: the scene was set for what became known as the 'July crisis' of 1966.

minister later recalled his view that the economy required a 'moderate disinflationary dose', similar to that administered a year earlier. But with clamour from all sides for urgent action, cabinet debate soon became polarised between those who supported Treasury plans for drastic deflation and those who felt the time had come to devalue sterling. In theory, the latter group constituted a formidable minority of ministers, including Brown, Crossman, Jenkins, Castle and Crosland. But in spite of resignation threats, the most senior of these figures, George Brown, was not inclined to give a firm lead, and instead added to the frenzied atmosphere by refusing to join colleagues in discussion.[23] In reality, the Prime Minister held the upper hand. He skilfully outmanoeuvred his opponents by stressing the damage devaluation would do to the Atlantic Alliance and by putting his personal authority on the line. 'Do you want me as Leader, Barbara?', Brown had plaintively asked, recognising that unless Wilson was openly challenged he could not beaten on such a major issue.[24] The result was a massive deflationary package aimed at demonstrating Labour's toughness to the financial markets. Cuts in public spending were accompanied by stiff increases in hire-purchase repayment terms and – much to the annoyance of trade unionists – a six month prices and wages freeze. Several economic commentators later claimed that the last opportunity of re-directing strategy by blaming devaluation on Tory mismanagement had been missed; others have argued that devaluation was not a panacea, and was only to be forced on the government by events that could not be foreseen in 1966.[25] What could not be doubted was the short-term impact of the 'July measures'. Labour MPs were stunned and dismayed by the severity of the cuts and by the effective abandonment of the much-vaunted National Plan. Instead of controlled growth, Chancellor Callaghan had turned his sights towards financial respectability and the reining in of consumer demand to hold back expansion. George Brown, who was moved from the DEA within weeks, reflected that 'it was undoubtedly the turning point; the point at which the Labour Party's attitude to life changed'.[26]

It was a certainly a turning point for Harold Wilson. From this moment on, disloyalty and distrust 'seemed to spread like some mysterious viral infection from the Prime Minister to his colleagues', slowly undermining the cabinet's sense of purpose and causing the government to 'slide further and further from the high ground of politics'.[27] The Labour leader may not, as Dick Crossman suggested in his diary, have suffered the most drastic decline of any post-war premier; but unlike Attlee – who recovered from his own low point in 1947 – Wilson was never the same force again.[28] Indeed worse was to come. At first it seemed that the July measures would do the trick. The pound steadied, monthly trade figures began to improve and the temporary pay freeze was superseded by a voluntary deal with the unions aimed at keeping down wage inflation. But within a year the situation deteriorated again. Deflation of the economy helped to push unemployment to its highest mid-year level since 1940, and renewed pressure on sterling was exacerbated by rumours abroad that Britain could not succeed in its bid to join the Common Market without realigning its currency. Urgent action once more became imperative. In November 1967 the cabinet finally faced up to the unavoidable: sterling was devalued by 14.3 per cent in relation to the dollar. Callaghan, conceding that he had gone back on his word, resigned as Chancellor, and was replaced by Roy Jenkins. The greatest humiliation was reserved for the Prime Minister, whose bizarre assertion that 'the pound in your pocket' remained unaffected was mercilessly exploited by the opposition.[29] Press commentators already had their knives out portraying devaluation as a national disaster when Wilson had to announce a fresh package of spending cuts. This meant, amongst other things, postponing plans to raise the school-leaving age and reintroducing prescription charges – the latter the most crushing blow of all for the man who had once resigned over the principle of free health care.

Devaluation also had knock-on consequences for Britain's position overseas. The government itself recognised early in 1966 the need to reduce defence spending, which at almost six per cent of gross national product was running far ahead of most western nations. But the Prime Minister, backed by Denis Healey as Defence Secretary, refused any dramatic cutbacks after his re-election, much to the annoyance of those in the party who felt domestic spending was suffering disproportionately. Only as the scale of the economic crisis unfolded in 1967 did Wilson face up to vitability of abandoning Britain's military bases east of ... This further setback for British national prestige helps to explain why, simultaneously, the Prime Minister began to modify Labour policy towards the European Community. He gradually came to the view that the weakness of sterling, combined with the diminishing importance of trading links with the Commonwealth, necessitated a fresh application for British membership. Over the winter of 1966–67 Wilson neatly managed to sidetrack opposition from those in the party who saw the Community as a 'rich man's club'. He also maintained cabinet unity, in spite of reservations from ministers doubting the economic benefits of membership; some never forgave his willingness to 'double-cross' those who stood in his way.[30] In the event, the Prime Minister's desire to 'dish the Tories' with an initiative that would provide a new theatre for British interests was frustrated when the French vetoed the application in May 1967. If this did nothing for the image Wilson hoped to cultivate with voters, then other aspects of foreign policy were causing increasing dismay in party ranks. Only a strong protest from MPs was enough, for example, to prevent ministers from relaxing Britain's arms embargo with South Africa. The *New Statesman* summed up the sense of alarm: 'a Labour Government that had sold armaments to South Africa would have ceased to be a Labour Government: it is as simple as that'.[31]

There was some comfort for Labour MPs on the domestic front after 1966. This was the period which saw the enactment of several of the legislative landmarks associated with the 'permissive society'. Amongst the most notable were measures to legalise both the termination of pregnancy, under certain conditions, and homosexuality between consenting adults. Other reforms aimed to bring Britain more into the European mainstream by updating the law on divorce, matrimonial property and equal pay. These measures produced only limited party conflict, but Labour opinion was clearly more willing to recognise how far societal attitudes had changed in recent years. The support of cabinet ministers was also vital. Unusually for measures that originated from private members, the Home Secretary, Roy Jenkins, both voiced his approval from the despatch box and ensured the availability of adequate parliamentary time. Without government backing, there would have been no 'liberal hour' in the 1960s.[32] For the most part, however, the impression persisted of an administration that was drifting from one crisis to another. A further illustration came early in 1968 over the question of the Kenyan Asians, arriving in large numbers as British passport holders after being forced out by the Kenyan authorities. In response to public concern, the government rushed through legislation tightening up immigration controls on those having 'no substantial connection' with the United Kingdom. Although balanced later in the year by an extension of race relations law, banning discrimination in areas such as housing and employment, the damage to party morale had already been done. After seeing tens of thousands of Kenyan Asians made homeless and stateless, recalls Roy Hattersley, 'there were a lot of *New Statesman* readers in suburban Britain who felt less willing to write the [local party] Ward minutes'.[33]

Nor did a tough line on immigration cut much ice with the wider electorate. Devaluation, tax increases and cuts to cherished social programmes such as free school milk took their toll on the government's popularity, which declined sharply from the heady days of March 1966. Aside from falling behind in the opinion polls, Labour suffered its worst local election defeats since before 1939, and by-election results pointed to an alarming loss of confidence. The Conservatives had lost only ten by-elections in their thirteen years of power. Wilson's government matched this in less than two years, losing supposedly 'safe' seats such as Dudley, which recorded a swing of over twenty per cent to the Tories. Altogether Labour was to lose sixteen of the 31 seats it defended: more than in the party's entire history since the turn of the century. 'No government in thirty years', notes David McKie, 'had experienced anything remotely like it.'[34] The sense of drift was unmistakable at all levels of the party. Local activists were staying at home rather than canvassing at election time, and despondency in the PLP was increasingly spilling over onto the floor of the Commons. Above all, the ebullient Prime Minister of 1964–65 had suddenly become a fugure of the past. Wilson now presided over an unhappy cabinet and was obsessed by adverse press coverage and rumours – real or imagined – of threats to his own position. Any talk of repeating the achievements of 1945 had quietly disappeared, and senior colleagues were under no illusions about how far the Prime Minister's horizons had narrowed, as Crossman observed in his diary:

> What are Harold's long-term economic objectives for this country? Does he want to go into Europe or doesn't he? I don't think he knows himself. . . . And what about the long term future of the Labour party? Does he see it as a real socialist party or does he, like the Gaitskellites, aim to turn it into an American Democratic Party or a German SPD? He certainly doesn't confide in me any profound thoughts about the future of the Labour party and I'm prepared to say as of today that I don't think he has them. . . . His aim is to stay in office. That's the real thing and for that purpose he will use any trick or gimmick.[35]

IV

Gimmicks did not come naturally to the minister most charged with keeping Wilson in power, Roy Jenkins. As Chancellor after 1967, with his reputation as a pioneering Home Secretary behind him, Jenkins was feared as much as admired by the Prime Minister. In the aftermath of devaluation, the balance of cabinet forces had altered. Callaghan's authority had been undermined, at least temporarily, by his resignation from the Treasury; and Wilson's other great rival of earlier years, George Brown, was removed from the running after finally acting upon one of his regular resignation threats early in 1968. Favourable press coverage for rising stars, such as Jenkins and Denis Healey, did nothing for Wilson's concern about the possibility of a 'palace revolt'. The Chancellor was not above suspicion, as he discovered after making an unauthorised speech that was particularly well-received. In an emotional outburst, the Prime Minister told colleagues that he knew 'where a great part of the leaking and backbiting comes from. It arises from the ambitions of one member of this Cabinet to sit in my place'.[36] While there was no foundation, at the time, in such claims, the circumstances in which Jenkins went to the Treasury did put him in a strong posisiton to dictate the course of economic policy. His overriding objective was soon identified as eliminating the balance of payments deficit; this, he believed, would show that devaluation had worked in restoring industrial competitiveness. In order to reach the promised land, Jenkins threatened 'two years' hard slog', and lived up to his word in April 1968 with the most deflationary budget ever seen in peacetime, increasing taxation by nearly a billion pounds. Labour MPs did not take kindly to the continued suppression of domestic demand and the further modification of spending plans. By the time that nearly 50 MPs voted against the reimposition of prescription charges, back-bench revolts had become an accepted feature of parliamentary life.

Ministers had generally ignored signs of unease among party supporters, such as annual conference defeats for the leadership after 1966 on a scale unknown in the Attlee years. But in 1969, just as the Chancellor was claiming to detect light at the end of the economic tunnel, the government went a step too far in provoking the party faithful. The occasion was an attempt to adjust Britain's industrial relations system, and the events that followed were to demonstrate how far the relationship between the political and industrial wings of the Labour movement had changed since 1945. Whereas wage restraint had been acceptable in the late 1940s in return for tangible benefits, by the 1960s pay policy was increasingly resented among rank-and-file trade unionists. Wilson's government, it was felt, looked for sacrifices from wage earners, and yet could guarantee neither full employment nor stable prices by way of compensation. While union leaders discussed the fine print of wage restraint, their membership was turning in larger numbers to the burgeoning shop stewards' movement. Hence an upsurge in unofficial strike activity which by 1967–68 left Britain with a poor record on industrial unrest. Lord Donovan's Royal Commission on trade unions reported in 1968 that legal sanctions against unofficial strikes would be unenforceable, though it did call for collective bargaining procedures to be voluntarily reformed. As incoming Secretary of State for Employment, Barbara Castle – hitherto a staunch supporter of the unions – decided to take up Lord Donovan's lead, a course also favoured by the Prime Minister. In Denis Healey's cynical view, 'Wilson came to the conclusion that his pay policy wasn't working, and didn't have public support, and therefore . . . he made a cold-blooded calculatation that he'd get more public support for a direct attack on union power through "In Place of Strife"'.[37]

Mrs Castle's White Paper, published in January 1969 as a precursor to legislation, was presented as a rational reform of industrial relations law, rather than as an open challenge to the unions. *In Place of Strife* proposed that the government be given powers to compel employers to negotiate with trade unions; those refusing to do so could be forced to accept arbitration and a legally binding award. But on the assumption that unions should have obligations as well as rights, Mrs Castle also proposed penal clauses not recommended by Donovan, such as a strike ballot before official stoppages and a compulsory cooling off period in certain industrial disputes.[38] Union leaders angrily denounced these penal clauses, the first of their kind suggested by any government since the war. The Labour left, especially those MPs in the recently-formed 'Tribune group', also saw here a straw that broke the camel's back. As Ian Mikardo recalled, it came on top of a prices and incomes policy that:

> . . . wasn't in fact a policy for prices and incomes – it was merely a policy for restricting increases in wages at the lower end of the scale. It was completely out of balance. . . . Unearned incomes, even the largest, were untouched by any semblance of restriction, and in earned incomes there was no restriction on professional earnings or managerial salaries: it was only the workers on the shop floor and in the offices, that is those in the lowest wage-brackets, who were to suffer limitations on increases in their pay packets. The document which Barbara had called . . . *In Place of Strife* was instead a provocation to strife.[39]

There was certainly no shortage of strife over the next few months. When the White Paper was discussed in parliament, 57 Labour MPs voted against the government, with at least 30 more abstaining. In order to forestall growing opposition, the Prime Minister decided to introduce a watered down version of the White Paper in the form of a short bill.

Wilson used all his guile in the weeks that followed. Behind the scenes, he tried to reasurre leaders of the Trades Union Congress (TUC) of the government's good faith. Publicly, his desperation showed in criticism of union leaders for wanting power without responsibility.[40] In reality, the odds were stacked against the Prime Minister. Back benchers were lukewarm about the idea of a short bill: some rejected penal legislation outright while others were more concerned about the imminent shattering of party unity. More important, cabinet support was starting to ebb away. Jim Callaghan, newly rehabilitated after his handling of unrest in Northern Ireland, took up the union cause in way that persuaded colleagues of his willingness to 'challenge Harold's leadership'.[41] In June Wilson and Mrs Castle were forced to beat a hasty retreat. The White Paper was dropped, and instead a face-saving formula was announced under which a 'solemn and binding' undertaking was given that member unions would observe the TUCs guidelines on regulating unofficial stoppages. The outcome was thus humiliation for the Prime Minister, especially as the TUCs lack of power to compel meant that its undertaking, 'though no doubt solemn, could hardly be described as binding'.[42] There could have been no clearer confirmation that Labour was unable to deliver on its promise to modernise the British economy – a point repeatedly hammered home by Edward Heath. Wilson had a point in blaming the result in part on union intransigence. 'I don't envy Ted having to deal with this crew', he commented, pointing to the possible electoral impact.[43] But he too was open to the charge that the ground had not been prepared thoroughly and that the loyalty of his own supporters had been tested once too often. For the first time since 1945, the efficacy of the political-industrial alliance had been called into question, and Labour had failed to resolve the question of whether it was to be the party of the unions or of the nation. 'The events surrounding the White Paper suggested that it might be neither.'[44]

After the pounding taken from all sides over industrial relations, the government's fortunes began to improve in the second half of 1969. At long last, the Chancellor had something to show for his policy of economic slog. Sterling had risen to its highest level for two years, interest rates had been reduced and the balance of payments position had been transformed, showing a large annual surplus by the beginning of 1970. Jenkins also rejected advice from colleagues that he should 'do a Maudling' – dash for growth in order to court short-term popularity – and in so doing took the credit for a politically astute budget in the spring. This included modest tax reductions while avoiding the charge of blatant electioneering. In an echo of Stafford Cripps, Jenkins pitched his offering along the lines that no further risks should be taken with the recovery now taking place. There were, however, many remaining weaknesses in the economy that cast doubt on the subsequent reputation of Jenkins as one of Britain's most successful post-war chancellors. Inflation had risen sharply since 1967 to reach 6.5 per cent; unemployment had increased by ten per cent in the same period; and growth in output turned out to be less than two per cent in both 1969 and 1970.[45] The achievement of a balance of payments surplus was nevertheless a potential election-winner. The opinion polls, which put Heath almost twenty per cent ahead at times, showed a steady narrowing of the gap by early 1970. After the budget and modest success in the local elections, Labour moved back into the lead. Wilson called an election for 18 June.

His reasoning was that to delay would be to miss his best opportunity of securing a third successive victory. As in the previous two campaigns, Wilson set the tone for Labour, this time presenting himself as the 'safety first' candidate, urging voters not to allow recovery to be jeopardised by the untried and extreme nostrums of the opposition. As in 1966, this meant seeking to exploit Edward Heath's stiff and uncomfortable television manner. 'He had not sung a duet with Edna Sharples at the *Sun* television awards dinner. He had not been on *Sportsnight with Coleman*.'[46] For much of the campaign this approach seemed to be working. Commentators and opinion polls combined to suggest a solid, if reduced, Labour majority. But in the final week there were signs of a shift in mood. Four days before polling, the government announced trade figures which, after nine months of surplus, showed a deficit of £31 million for May. This appeared to strengthen one of Heath's main arguments: namely that there was no sound basis to Labour's so-called economic recovery. The Chancellor later recollected his feeling that 'this one might be slipping away from us', but he like most others was stunned to find that the result produced 'defeat out of the jaws of victory'.[47] On the largest uniform swing at any post-war election, the Conservatives were returned to power with a majority of 30 over all other parties. Labour lost a total of 70 seats, mostly in the south-east, the Midlands and the north-west, and its share of the vote fell back to 1959 levels. There was broad agreement that this was an election as much 'lost' by the government as 'won' by the appeal of the opposition. Lack of enthusiasm amongst voters was reflected in the lowest turnout since 1935, and if there was any significant swing in the last few days, it could only have occurred with the electorate in an uncertain state of mind. In the end, the Tories triumphed in this 'unpopularity contest' because the 'family doctor', Harold Wilson, 'for all his reassuring skills, had not quite succeeded in healing the scar tissue over the wounds of 1966 to 1969'.[48]

V

Wilson had not managed to emulate Attlee. Douglas Jay, who served both Prime Ministers, was in no doubt about their relative merits: 'The comparative failure of the 1964 Wilson government, by contrast with the Attlee government of 1945–51, is startling.'[49] This is not to say that future historians will have difficulty in finding good things to say about Labour's record in the 1960s. In several areas of national life the 1964 government sought to follow the example of its 1945 predecessor in helping the underdog. It had introduced equal pay for women and a statutory right to redundancy pay; it had made the first serious attempt to curb racism in British society; it had created the Open University and encouraged a massive opening-up of opportunities in higher education, both at the universities and the newly-created polytechnics; and it had helped to ensure that a third of the nation's school-children were now in comprehensive schools, so avoiding the stigma of being branded 'secondary modern failures' at the age of eleven.[50] Wilson's administration had also used the benefits system to help the less well-off, for example by increasing old age pensions, doubling the level of family allowances and introducing rent rebates for nearly a million householders. In addition to direct payments, many benefits in kind were received as public expenditure rose sharply. Despite the various cutbacks after 1966, spending on services such as health and education was still much higher as a proportion of national wealth than it had been when Labour came to power. And in raising taxes to pay for these reforms, careful attention was paid to principle of redistribution: disposable income rose for the lowest paid while falling amongst the wealthiest.[51] All of this would have been recognisable to Attlee's cabinet and could be interpreted as continuing the party's tradition of progressive social change. Indeed, when combined with the liberalising reforms of the late 1960s, the Wilson years for some might seem to constitute a golden age.

The sense of failure nevertheless persists. In the minds of both the public and party members, the 1964 government – unlike Attlee's administration – did not leave behind a readily defensible legacy. The Prime Minister got little credit with voters for scaling down Britain's global commitments; if anything loss of world prestige was compounded by his futile efforts to secure membership of the European Community. He got even less credit from Labour activists appalled by the lengths to which he would go in order to preserve the Atlantic Alliance. Support for the bombing of Vietnamese peasants was one of only several examples. The physical removal of the inhabitants of Diego Garcia in the Indian Ocean – uprooted from their tiny island to make way for an American military base – was another case in point. On the home front, the government's economic difficulties were equally damaging. Working-class supporters especially were alienated by higher taxation at a time of wage restraint and spiralling prices in the shops: they demonstrated their displeasure by staying at home in large numbers at the 1970 election.[52] Party workers, for their part, were dismayed to find that any increases in public spending were given a much lower priority than tackling the balance of payments deficit. With unemployment and inflation at record post-war levels by 1970, Wilson's optimism about a technological revolution had become a distant memory. The prospect of modernisation through central planning had been mocked by the impotence of Labour's administrative machinery, notably the defunct DEA, and by the retreat to orthodox Treasury remedies. With increases in industrial output averaging no more than two per cent per year, it was difficult to avoid the charge – as one minister subsequently conceded – that the Wilson government had sacrificed economic growth for an unsustainable exhange rate and an untenable incomes policy.[53]

Many of the government's problems were either inherited or intractable. As the Conservative experience before 1964 testified, there was no obvious way of escaping the reality of a low-growth, low investment economy, struggling to keep pace with the likes of Germany and Japan as Britain's influence overseas withered away. In some ways, Wilson could argue that the obstacles he faced were greater than those of his predecessors. The wartime inheritance of full employment, for example, could no longer be guaranteed in a world of changing trading patterns, and Labour also had to contend with pressures to recognise changed social conventions that had been largely absent in the 1950s. In addition, as Wilson himself liked to emphasise, his best efforts were constantly at the mercy of the financial markets, who remained throughout the period intensely suspicious of Labour's welfare programme.[54] But none of this explains away the failure of leadership that characterised the 1964 government. The burden of guilt rests to an extent with the whole cabinet. In spite of individual resignations, ministers were mostly prepared to go along with policies that damaged Labour's credibility, such as the fateful decision to deflate rather than devalue in July 1966. Above all though, it was the Prime Minister – the chief architect of the 1966 election victory – whose stewardship had increasingly debilitating effects. His deviousness was the root cause of much avoidable intrigue around the cabinet table; as Tony Crosland put it, 'one hasn't the faintest idea whether the bastard means what he says even at the moment he speaks it'.[55] More serious, he proved unable to provide any form of coherent medium-term strategy that would bind together and sustain both government and party. In the scathing words of Denis Healey, one of the ministers with whom Wilson remained on generally good terms:

He had no sense of direction, and rarely looked more than a
few months ahead. His short-term opportunism, allied with a
capacity for self-delusion which made Walter Mitty appear
unimaginative, often plunged the government into chaos.
Worse still, when things went wrong he imagined everyone was
conspiring against him. . . . The steady deterioration of the
economy following his victory in 1966 led him to see enemies in
every corner; at worst he began to behave, in the words of an
uncharitable journalist, like 'a demented coypu'.[56]

In view of these failings, Wilson must shoulder the lion's share of
responsibility, if not for the nation's economic plight, then at least
for the damage his premiership inflicted on the Labour movement.
When he departed from Downing Street, the unity of the early
1960s had evaporated. A resurgence of left-right tension inside the
PLP was symptomatic of several disturbing trends. Away from
Westminster in the constituencies, demoralised party members
drifted away in unprecedented numbers. The fall in individual
membership, down to 680,000 since 1964, was almost as great as in
whole thirteen-year period after 1951. Under Wilson's leadership,
'the grass', it was said, 'came away from the roots'; there were signs
that the participation of working-class supporters in party activity
was perceptibly declining.[57] Equally worrying were consequences
of the Prime Minister's abortive attempt to 'do something' about
the trade unions. By failing to prepare the ground adequately and
attempting reform too late in his term of office, Wilson went further
even than Hugh Gaitskell in offending party sentiment. 'The Social
Democratic dilemma – how to contain the interests of organised
labour within a broadly-based political party, and how to combine
free trade unionism with the efficient management of a mixed
economy – remained unresolved.'[58] Instead, Wilson undermined
his own credibility by pointing up his government's inability to
reconcile free collective bargaining with economic growth. In this
sense *In Place of Strife* was a contributory factor in the outcome of
the 1970 election; a crushing defeat which, with hindsight, was far
more damaging than the reverses of the 1950s. There was now
firmer evidence that the manual working class as a proportion of
the total electorate was beginning to shrink at the expense of white-

collar, professional groups, though there was no compelling reason why this should cause Labour to lose ground within its core constituency. And yet voters' survey evidence suggests that in 1970 support for the party fell by ten times the amount that could be expected on the basis of social change – an indication of deep disaffection just at the moment when class was beginning to be less salient in determining voter choice.[59]

In one final respect, the disillusionment of voters and activists pointed to a deeper malaise, putting into perspective the crucial disjuncture between the Attlee and Wilson eras. In both instances loss of power sharpened ideological divisions. Just as the election defeat of 1951 had led to hostility between Bevanites and Gaitskellites, so the unexpected reverse in 1970 was followed by renewed in-fighting between the inheritors of the old fundamentalist and revisionist traditions. But the arguments of the 1970s were to be conducted in a markedly different framework. Wilson's premiership had left a legacy of uncertainty. His style of leadership – in which 'public relations superseded public planning, tactics swamped strategy, and cosmetics dominated economics'[60] – made it difficult to know what Labour really stood for any longer. How could it be party of science when technology had failed to transform the economy? How could it be the party of revisionism when glaring social inequalities still remained? How could it be the party of fundamentalist socialism when no major extensions of public ownership had taken place? And how could it be the party of organised labour when so many trade unionists had become disaffected? This confusion about the party's identity was compounded by a recognition that Labour was now on the defensive to a greater extent than at any time since the war. In spite of successive defeats at the polls in the 1950s, the party faithful – looking back to both the record and the integrity of the Attlee government – could trust that, one day, the forward march of the progressive left would inevitably be resumed. This spirit of optimism, if not destroyed, was much harder to detect when Harold Wilson left office. 'The road to Jerusalem, it seemed, was not open after all; perhaps it did not even exist'.[61]

4

'CRISIS. WHAT CRISIS?', 1970–79

I

'As it began, so it ends. The decade from 1970 to 1979 entered, and left, to the sound of Labour Governments falling.' These were the opening words of Ken Coates in *What Went Wrong*, a collection of essays published by the Institute of Workers Control shortly after Labour's crushing defeat at the 1979 general election.[1] Few have challenged the claim in *What Went Wrong* – intended as a statement rather than a question – that the Labour administration of 1974–79 failed even more miserably than its 1960s predecessor. For those on the Labour left, such as Coates, the central theme of these years was the systematic abandonment in office of socialist policies developed by the party whilst in opposition during the early 1970s. Even those who served in the 1974–79 government have been reluctant to defend their record, accepting that serious mistakes were made, especially in the conduct of economic affairs.[2] Many of the wider, public perceptions about the period – which were still to have electoral resonance over a decade later – stemmed from the images conjured up by a hostile press, anxious to depict Britain as being ungovernable and on the verge of collapse. In the eyes of the tabloid newspapers, this was the era of rampant inflation, rising above twenty per cent in the mid-1970s to become the great public enemy; of ministers so mishandling events that Britain had to be 'bailed out' by the International Monetary Fund (IMF); and of the dead going unburied, as overmighty trade unionists orchestrated the 'winter of discontent' in 1979. If the performance of Labour in the 1960s had been disappointing, then what followed in the 1970s could be described as 'pitiable'. Almost negligible growth, record inflation and a rise in unemployment that made nonsense of post-war assumptions about economic management – this was a record that 'ranks as one of the worst of the century'.[3]

There were, it must be said, mitigating circumstances. When Harold Wilson returned to power in 1974, he was faced with an appalling 'dual inheritance'. On the one hand, the British economy was in a far worse condition than in the 1960s, partly as a result of failures by the 1970–74 Heath government, and partly because of external pressures following the world oil crisis. On the other hand, Wilson's room for manoeuvre was further limited by political factors. He had to contend, for example, with a more overtly socialist programme than he hoped for at a time when the government had no adequate working majority in parliament. In many respects no post-war Prime Minister had come into power facing more daunting prospects.[4] Nor did the context in which the government operated improve over time. Wilson's successor as Prime Minister in 1976, James Callaghan, found it necessary to construct a pact with the Liberal party simply to continue in office, and as economic difficulties intensified, there was no shortage of opposition to Labour's programme from powerful vested interests – industrial firms and spokesmen for business, senior civil servants and international financial agencies.[5] In recognition of these constraints, the outline of a revisionist interpretation of the 1970s has begun to emerge. Denis Healey has provided a typically pugnacious defence of the economic record, and some recent studies maintain that judgements on the 1974–79 government have been distorted and unfair, often for partisan political reasons.[6] What seems more difficult to dispute was that Labour's leadership, preoccupied with the breakdown of Britain's post-war settlement, proved unable to prevent growing disaffection in party ranks, brought to a head and intensified by the nature and scale of the election defeat in 1979. By the end of the decade Labour was a party in crisis; its continued existence as a viable political force called into question.

II

Labour entered opposition in June 1970 facing an uncertain future. The party needed a convincing new programme if it was to win back disillusioned voters; at the same time efforts would have to be made to mend fences with the trade unions. For much of the term of the Heath government that followed, these tasks looked to be beyond Harold Wilson. After winning two out of three elections, Wilson remained secure as leader. But he was unable to provide anything like the enthusiasm and guidance of the early 1960s. Indeed he spent his first six months out of office writing up his 'personal record' of the 1964 government, with the result that Labour made a poor public showing. Members of the largely unchanged front-bench team followed the example of MPs in squabbling over the causes of defeat and the remedies required. Nor was the opposition's task made any easier by mounting industrial unrest, which kept the 'union problem' at the forefront of public attention. Heath's determination to control public sector wages and to introduce tough trade union legislation helped to provoke an atmosphere of militancy not seen since the 1920s. Unions led by the miners showed themselves willing both to take on the government – humiliating Heath after a successful six-week strike in 1972 – and to employ aggressive picketing techniques. Press attempts to exploit this situation by accusing Labour of supporting extra-parliamentary activity made it imperative that fresh attempts were made to revive the party-union alliance. By 1973 it was clear that a future Labour administration would seek consensus rather than further confrontation with the unions. The announcement of a new 'compact' went a long way to restoring harmony by committing the party to price controls and the repeal of Heath's hated Industrial Relations Act, the penal provisions of which went well beyond *In Place of Strife*. But any electoral advantage that Wilson hoped to gain was mitigated by the ambiguity of the compact on incomes; in spite of much hard bargaining, union leaders refused to commit themselves in advance to formal wage restraint.[7]

There were greater problems, moreover, in other areas of policy formation. The first two years of opposition were overshadowed by protracted disputes over the party's attitude towards the European Community. A minority of pro-Market MPs, mainly from the revisionist wing of the party, backed Edward Heath in securing British entry, despite growing scepticism at grass-roots level about the benefits of membership. In an effort to reconcile divisions, Wilson adopted a compromise: Labour would renegotiate the terms of entry and hold a referendum on British membership – a formula which prompted the resignation from the front-bench of the Shadow Chancellor, Roy Jenkins.[8] In retrospect, this was a serious blow to the Labour right, especially as the staunchly pro-European views of Jenkins and his acolytes were not shared by another leading revisionist, Tony Crosland. 'Their idea of a Labour Party is not mine', confided Crosland to his wife; 'Roy has come actually to dislike socialism'.[9] Fragmentation on the right meant that the Labour left was able to make the running in a way that had been impossible in the 1950s and 1960s. The disenchantment of local activists with Wilson's record in office was reflected both in the composition of the constituency section of the NEC and in conference demands that the leadership be made more accountable. For the first time since the death of Bevan, rank-and-file members could also look to an inspirational figurehead. In the words of Philip Whitehead: 'There came out to join them Tony Benn, once the youthful technocrat of the first Wilson era, now a born-again socialist radicalised by his experience of workers in struggle.'[10] The clearest indication of increased left-wing influence came with the adoption of *Labour's Programme 1973*, which called for major extensions of public ownership and greater state intervention in the planning of private enterprise. Wilson, fearing the electoral consequences, sought to play down expectations and announced that he would veto the idea of taking a controlling interest in 'twenty five of our largest manufacturers'.[11]

Labour did not therefore paint an inspiring picture in opposition. The public face of the party was one of confusion and dissent, under a leader who seemed to promise 'a better yesterday rather than a more fruitful tomorrow'.[12] Interviewed by journalists in 1972 about his future plans if returned to power, Wilson replied that his top priority was to deal with his 'enemies', the political correspondents of the main newspapers.[13] By failing to give a strong lead, Wilson had saddled himself with a policy package in which he had little faith and had permitted the ambitions of the left to go unchecked. The problems this might raise were brought into sharp focus in 1973 when constituency workers in Lincoln refused to readopt the revisionist Dick Taverne for a by-election. With strong backing from the press, Taverne handsomely defeated the official candidate under an independent label, basing his case on Labour's growing 'extremism'. The Lincoln by-election highlighted how – in stark contrast to the early 1960s – Labour was unable to make much electoral headway against an unpopular Tory administration. The party made only one by-election gain after 1970 and found itself vulnerable to a rise in support for both the Liberals and the Scottish Nationalists. Aside from being unable to establish any lasting lead in the opinion polls, Labour's own private research demonstrated widespread public scepticism about policies such as further nationalisation.[14] In the event, the party's full programme was put to the test much sooner than anticipated. In the wake of a deteriorating economic situation, compounded by another miners' strike and the need to introduce a three-day working week, Heath decided that his only option was to call a general election in February 1974.

Labour hopes were not high as the campaign got under way. The party had visibly been at odds with itself – rather like the early 1950s – and the circumstances of the election seemed to favour the government. In the early stages, Heath made the running with a clear message: that the nation should be governed by its elected representatives and not 'held to ransom' by the miners. Labour was fiercely criticised in the press for producing its most radical manifesto since 1945. In addition to major extensions of public ownership, promised on the grounds of improving economic efficiency, the party pledged itself to a new Wealth Tax and sweeping extensions of welfare services. But as the campaign progressed, the tide appeared to turn. Heath found it difficult to sustain for three weeks his single 'Who Governs?' theme, and he looked susceptible to a sharp rise in opinion poll support for the

Liberals. Wilson, meanwhile, was plugging away at the Conservative record on inflation and unemployment since 1970. This left Jim Callaghan – the staunch friend of the unions over *In Place of Strife* – to draw Heath's fire by reassuring trade unionists and the wider public that only Labour could effectively deal with the miners. Such a strategy paid off after the government's own Pay Board admitted that miners were not so high up the league of industrial earnings as had been suggested. From this point on, Wilson was able to claim with greater confidence that the miseries of the three-day week had more to do with government incompetence than with workers' intransigence.[15] When the votes came to be counted, the outcome was as close as many were predicting in the last few days of campaigning. Labour emerged as the largest party with four more seats than the Conservatives, but in the first hung parliament since 1929, the balance of power rested with the minor parties. After unsuccessfully attempting to secure Liberal support, Heath resigned. Harold Wilson returned to Downing Street, this time to form a minority government.

The result was hardly a ringing endorsement of the Labour party. Its 37 per cent share of the vote was remarkably low by post-war standards; indeed with half a million less supporters than in 1970, Labour actually polled fewer votes than the Tories. In practice both the major parties had suffered an unprecedented drop in support. The main beneficiary of the 'plague on both your houses' attitude among voters was the Liberal party, whose share of the vote had risen from seven to nineteen per cent.[16] With political commentators focusing on the shock administered to the traditional two-party system, it was widely agreed that the 1974 parliament would be short-lived. Nor was it electoral circumstances alone that limited Labour's room for manoeuvre. Party activists still harboured thoughts of radical departures in policy. Many on the left believed the manifesto heralded more far-reaching socialist policies than attempted in the 1960s, while revisionists such as Crosland hoped that if ministers chose the right priorities – such as devaluation rather than deflation – then economic growth and redistribution could be achieved.[17] But Wilson's sights were set rather lower. He was conscious that the constraints upon policy-makers were far greater than when he first became Prime Minister back in 1964. In the domestic arena, a belated 'dash for growth' by Heath had again left a legacy of rising inflation, at a time when the unions were in no mood to commit themselves to wage restraint. This was without the shock-waves that followed on the wider international stage after a fourfold rise in oil prices during 1973; the further sharp twist in the inflation spiral that loomed as a result had already prompted some of the major Western economies to tighten up their fiscal and monetary policies. Political and economic circumstances thus combined to ensure that Wilson's priorities were once more short-term: how could Labour stabilise the economy and win another election?

III

Wilson acted swiftly and decisively. He ignored speculation about possible parliamentary deals to bolster Labour's position, and instead appointed a cabinet that combined old hands with new blood. The centre-right once again dominated, with Callaghan as Foreign Secretary, Jenkins at the Home Office and Denis Healey promoted to the Treasury; this was balanced by the appointment to key economic posts of Tony Benn and Michael Foot, the latter regarded as a custodian of the party's socialist conscience. Within days of coming to power, the Prime Minister had also settled the miners' strike and brought to an end the official state of emergency. In the medium-term, matters were not so straightforward. The government next had to demonstrate that it had some means of tackling run-away inflation, a record balance of payments deficit, and the scars of the three-day week. Aware that the other parties were unlikely to combine to force another election immediately, the Prime Minister decided to press ahead with an economic programme containing two main elements. Heath's policy of compulsory wage restraint was scrapped and replaced by statutory price controls and the 'Social Contract', an attempt to confront inflationary pressures through voluntary agreements with the unions. In addition, Chancellor Healey decided to adopt a mildly expansionist budgetary policy, borrowing heavily to subsidise food prices and to finance increased pensions – one of Labour's manifesto commitments. Other nations were already cutting expenditure to counter the impact of massive oil price increases, and Healey's approach has been much criticised, even by those involved in the decision making process. Joel Barnett, the Chancellor's deputy at the Treasury, later described the policy as 'spending money which in the event we did not have'.[18] At the time, however, there were few viable alternatives. To have opted for deflation, as senior ministers realised, would have undermined the government's popularity and jeopardised the new departure of the Social Contract.[19]

The whole economic strategy was geared to the likelihood of an early election. By holding down inflation to reasonable levels, the government succeeded in producing a modest improvement in living standards. Against this background, and conscious that little more in the way of legislation could be pushed through, the Prime Minister brought to an end the shortest parliament since 1681. Two elections in the same year did nothing to stimulate voter interest: the turnout in October 1974 was to slump by more than two million from the February level. Nor was there much excitement in a campaign dominated by familiar faces. Seeking distraction, the press turned the spotlight on the novel hovercraft campaign embarked upon by Jeremy Thorpe, the Liberal leader. ' "I'm Jeremy Thorpe," he announced to one holidaymaker. "That's your problem not mine!" ' was the dour reply. The hovercraft sank at Sidmouth.'[20] Edward Heath's attempt to adopt a more concil-iatory tone was undermined by right-wing calls to abandon Keynesian economics in favour of monetarism; the admission that this might temporarily push up unemployment, before control of the money supply worked its way through in tackling inflation, led to accusations that the Tories were 'the party of unemployment'. This left Labour to keep its nose in front by stressing the same theme as in 1966: that a clear mandate was needed to carry out its full programme. In the event, the 1966 pattern of a 'follow-up' victory was only partially repeated. A swing of two per cent was enough to give Labour an overall majority, though by the slender margin of only three seats. Wilson could celebrate a unique four election victories from five contests, and the Conservatives once again looked like the declining force in British politics. But Labour's share of the poll was the lowest for any majority government since 1922, and its performance in suburban marginals was well below the national average. The number of Labour voters had fallen since February, and the steadiness of Liberal support suggested that disenchantment with both the main parties was still widespread.[21] If 1966 had been a wasted opportunity, 1974 might be a last chance to make Labour the natural party of government.

For several months, a parliamentary majority of three was more secure than it looked at first sight. Labour had won 43 more seats than the Conservatives, and there were few indications of the opposition parties acting in unison to embarrass the government. This helps to explain how the Prime Minister emerged unscathed from the most contentious issue in the early period of his new premiership: British membership of the European Community. Along with his Foreign Secretary, Jim Callaghan, Wilson set about fulfilling the party's manifesto pledge by negotiating fresh terms. These fell well short of the changes demanded by Labour activists, but with majority support in the cabinet, the Prime Minister went ahead in recommending acceptance of the terms in a referendum on British membership in June 1975. In an effort to assuage anti-market sentiment, Wilson took the unusual step of allowing ministers to waive collective responsibility and participate in a 'Britain out' movement that crossed party lines. Anti-marketeers were less convinced, however, that the party machinery remained neutral as promised, and their fears were borne out when the referendum produced a two-one majority in favour of remaining inside the EEC.[22] Unlike trade union reform in 1969, where the leadership had been similarly opposed by mainstream opinion within the party, Wilson's handling of events this time paid off. By allowing differences to be openly expressed, and by holding a referendum that made the debate largely external to the party, the Prime Minister succeeded in what he had always been best at: maintaining unity. Pro-Europeans such as Roy Jenkins took comfort from the result while anti-marketeers like Tony Benn accepted that voters had been given the chance to deliver their verdict.[23] With the exception of the referendum, foreign policy grabbed few of the headlines in 1975. For the most part, Callaghan continued to enhance his reputation by steady diplomacy. In particular, he was able to cement the Atlantic Alliance by working closely with Henry Kissinger, the American Secretary of State, confident in the knowledge that – Europe aside – overseas affairs were less divisive within Labour ranks as Vietnam receded in memory. The same could not be said of the issue that inevitably returned to the forefront – the crisis in the British economy.

With the prospect of a reasonable term of office ahead, Denis Healey continued with the main lines of economic policy laid down before the October 1974 election. In essence, this meant relying on the Social Contract to ensure 'sensible' wage bargaining in return for extended welfare benefits, to be paid for by redistributive taxation and large-scale borrowing. Over the winter of 1974–75, the Chancellor made optimistic speeches about breaking out of the stagflationary spiral of low productivity and high inflation, and he continued to raise welfare spending as promised. But it was not long before a rethink became necessary. As world recession deepened, British exports suffered; growth in the economy fell sharply; unemployment rose and inflation at over twenty per cent seemed to be veering out of control. In practice, the Social Contract did not succeed in holding wage increases below the level of price rises. As one minister was to sourly observe, 'the only give and take in the contract was that the Government gave and the unions took'.[24] During the spring of 1975, at a time when cabinet ministers were preoccupied with the European referendum, Healey decided there was no option but to reverse the engines. His 'rough and tough' April budget raised income tax to 35p in the pound and slashed spending programmes by £900 million, with major economies in defence and in price subsidies for the nationalised industries. Cabinet colleagues reluctantly fell into line. Left-wing members who complained that such a package made a mockery of workers receiving a 'social wage' were told that the unions had already killed the Social Contract; those on the right who complained about accepting 'orthodox Treasury deflation' were asked to come up with an alternative. 'The party', conceded Tony Crosland, a cabinet sceptic now charged with cutting deep into local authority spending, 'is over'.[25]

Many on the left saw this re-run of July 1966 as a betrayal of Labour's manifesto commitments, a charge that was repeated when Tony Benn was removed as Industry Secretary in June 1975.

Benn had argued strongly for a new National Enterprise Board, as agreed under the 1973 programme, to spearhead state-led economic recovery, but found his colleagues would consent to no more than a series of rescue operations for 'lame-duck' industries. Although the public sector continued to expand, the Industry Secretary also received little support for his ambitious plans to impose planning agreements on private firms. By exploiting the defeat of the 'no' campaign in the European referendum – with which Benn was closely identified – the Prime Minister was able to isolate his troublesome colleague by moving him to the energy department. Wilson had thus fulfilled his aim of circumventing undesirable aspects of the 'new industrial strategy' promised in 1974. This was followed in July by a further indication of the government's change of direction. Recognising the ineffectiveness of the Social Contract, ministers announced the introduction of a formal – though still voluntary – pay policy, holding down wage increases across the board. By announcing a freeze on higher salaries, the Chancellor hoped to placate critics who argued that it was the lowest paid who suffered most from economic retrenchment. Healey was claiming success within months: wage increases slowed and inflation was finally on a downward trend. Nevertheless, both his and the government's popularity took a battering. The combination of a return to deflation, the introduction of 'cash limits' on public expenditure and the emasculation of Tony Benn's industrial strategy caused outrage on the Labour left, led by the Tribune group. Amidst cries of 'selling out', the Chancellor was ousted from the NEC, and the left-right tensions of the early 1970s began to resurface openly in public. Voters also registered their disapproval. With unemployment rising sharply, living standards depressed and public spending running well ahead of output, Labour's poll rating started to plummet. All the signs pointed to a repeat of the mid-1960s, with a Labour administration drifting aimlessly from one crisis measure to another. 'It was like being on the sinking Titanic', recalls one insider, 'although without the music'.[26]

After narrowly surviving a vote of 'no confidence' in the spring of 1976, Harold Wilson surprised the nation by announcing his retirement. Political commentators, stunned by this bolt from the blue, speculated that he had been 'forced out'. Some argued that he wished to abandon the sinking ship before it hit an economic iceberg; others were close to the mark in suggesting that Wilson's decision was partly prompted by a secret campaign of destabilisation waged by elements of the security services.[27] But in the main, the Prime Minister's motives were quite mundane. He had repeatedly told his closest advisers of his intention to retire around the age of sixty, and as he noted in his resignation speech, he wanted to leave his successor sufficient time to make a mark in the present parliament. The events of the past two years had added little to Wilson's reputation. His style had become more relaxed than in the 1960s; in footballing terms he had played less as a centre forward and more as a 'deep-lying centre half'.[28] He had also managed to maintain the party's precarious unity on contentious areas of policy such as Europe, though only at a price. Wilson's desire not to rock the boat had left key issues unresolved. His relaxed approach to party management had opened up the possibility of 'entryism' by extremist groupings, and factional differences were allowed to simmer beneath the surface: 'just as he did not wish to be educated by his party, so he gave up trying to educate it'.[29] This was no easy inheritance for the former elementary school-boy, Jim Callaghan, who defeated five Oxford graduates in the contest for the leadership that followed. On the final ballot, support from the centre-right of the PLP was sufficent to ensure comfortable victory over the main challenger from the left, Michael Foot. In his first broadcast to the nation from No. 10 Downing Street, Callaghan made a sober assessment of Britain's economic prospects, emphasising in particular the dangers of high inflation. There could be no greater contrast between this and Wilson's promises about the 'scientific revolution' when he assumed the leadership back in 1963. As events were soon to prove, the new Prime Minister had every reason to play down expectations.

IV

In some respects Callaghan was from the same mould as Wilson. The son of a naval chief petty officer, he too was a pragmatic politician, less concerned with ideology than with common sense solutions to everyday problems. Perhaps more so than any previous Labour leader, 'Callaghan offered "safety first" natural and unashamed'.[30] He could also boast, like his predecessor, a strong personal following when taking over as Prime Minister. Within the Labour movement, he was regarded as a particular friend of the trade unions, having served as a union official in his early career. As far as the wider public were concerned, Callaghan came across as an avuncular, trustworthy figure; the 'able seaman' who could navigate choppy economic waters. There were nevertheless important differences between the two Labour leaders. In contrast to Wilson's evasiveness, Callaghan's style of leadership was far more direct. As one colleague put it, he 'always had a clear view of what he wanted to get out of a cabinet discussion, and he guided the discussion in his direction'; on occasion this was to reveal a bullying manner that belied his 'Sunny Jim' image.[31] He was thus a more effective manager of business than Wilson, and for the next three years the cabinet was to be more harmonious and free of conspiracy than it had been in the 1960s. Callaghan was also able to build up closer working relationships: notably with Denis Healey, who continued as Chancellor, and with Michael Foot, whose importance as a spokesman of the left was recognised by his role as Leader of the House of Commons. More so than his predecessor, the new premier had been lucky in his rise to the top. But for the timing of Wilson's resignation, allege his critics, Callaghan would have been too old to take over, and would have been remembered as a figure of limited vision with a mixed ministerial career behind him.[32] His good fortune did not, however, look as though it would long survive his arrival in Downing Street. In addition to his inheritance of a tiny parliamentary majority and a party at odds with itself, Callaghan was faced within months by the gravest economic crisis since 1931.

The spring of 1976 was dominated by a renewed sterling crisis. Chancellor Healey had made several vain efforts to persuade the financial markets of his prudence. He announced further spending cuts early in 1976 and introduced a fiscally prudent budget in April; this was followed up by stage two of the government's voluntary incomes policy. But the pound continued to slide, helped on its way by a bungled Treasury attempt to engineer a controlled devaluation as a means of boosting British exports. With currency reserves disappearing in an effort to prop up sterling, Treasury officials made it clear that Healey faced a stark choice: either further cuts to restore city confidence, or else turning to the IMF, which was itself certain to insist upon draconian cutbacks as the price of outside assistance. The Chancellor opted for another 'July package', this time reducing public spending by a billion pounds and raising interest rates to record levels. Cabinet ministers reluctantly accepted that there was no alternative, though doubters such as Crosland, Callaghan's replacement as Foreign Secretary, were under no illusions about the implications:

(a) Demoralisation of decent rank and file. . . . (b) Strain on TU loyalty. . . . (c) breeding of illiterate and reactionary attitude to public expenditure – horrible. (d) collapse of strategy which I proposed last year . . . Now no sense of direction and no priorities; only pragmatism, empiricism, safety first, £ supreme. (e) and: unemployment = grave loss of welfare, security, choice; very high price to be paid for deflation and negative growth.[33]

In the event, Healey ended up with the worst of all worlds. He had gone too far in the eyes of many party members, making long-standing enemies in the process by accusing his critics of being 'out of their tiny Chinese minds'. What was worse, in the short-term, his deflationary medicine had not restored city confidence. 'The markets wanted blood', recalled one insider, and the July package 'didn't look like blood'.[34] The fall in sterling continued.

By September, the Chancellor believed there was no option but to announce his intention to apply for an IMF stand-by loan. As negotiations got under way, it was clear the IMF would drive a hard bargain: in return for financial aid, the government would have to cut £2.5 billion from the Public Sector Borrowing Requirement over two years, sell off £500 million of British Petroleum shares, and ensure strict control of the money supply. In order to secure acceptance of these terms, the Prime Minister skilfully allowed any alternative proposals to be exhaustively discussed in cabinet. Tony Benn's advocacy of an 'alternative economic strategy', including import controls and further nationalisation, was savaged by his opponents as being pie in the sky.[35] This left the more cogently argued objections of revisionist ministers, led by Crosland, who claimed that there was no economic justification for further 'meat-axe' cuts, which were being demanded solely in order to steady the foreign exchanges. When Callaghan finally threw his weight behind the Chancellor, Crosland gave way. 'This is nonsense, but we must do it', he concluded, realising that to oppose the Prime Minister would split the party down the middle and ensure the break up of the government.[36] On 15 December, Healey finally announced the details of the IMF agreement to the House of Commons; he was greeted with disbelief on his own side and derision from the Conservatives benches, led by Heath's successor as party leader, Margaret Thatcher. Despite the ridicule to which he was subjected in the press, Callaghan could take some satisfaction from the outcome. He had managed to hold together, in daunting circumstances, both the cabinet and the PLP, who were forced to face up to the choice of cuts or the likelihood of a Tory election victory. But an enormous price had been paid. Denis Healey had jeopardised his prospects of one day becoming party leader; it was not only the Tribunite left who believed he had been too willing to do the dirty work of the IMF and the US Treasury.[37] What remained of the revisionist right was equally shattered: the ideals of economic growth and social equality as favoured by Crosland – who died unexpectedly a few months later – seemed further away than ever. The government's humiliation also had its effect on the voting public. Labour fell way behind in the opinion polls, and lost two by-elections in rapid succession, at Workington and Walsall North, the latter on a swing that suggested a return to the dismal days of the late 1960s. As if to complete Callaghan's baptism of fire as Prime Minister, by early 1977 the government had lost its overall parliamentary majority.

By a mixture of skill and good fortune, Callaghan survived and began to fight back in 1977. Those who predicted the imminent collapse of the government during the IMF crisis were confounded by two main developments. In the first place, the Prime Minister managed to secure a political breathing space. Seeking to avoid an early election, which looked certain to result in defeat, Callaghan entered into negotiations with the new Liberal leader, David Steel. The resultant 'Lib-Lab pact' first became public knowledge when the Liberals sided with the government to defeat an opposition motion of 'no confidence' in March. Both parties to the agreement claimed success. Callaghan was content that he had secured a more stable parliamentary base without making major concessions. He knew that the Liberals – trying to recover from the resignation of Jeremy Thorpe after accusations involving conspiracy to murder a male model – were equally keen to avoid an election, and consequently he refused to countenance Liberal demands such as a referendum on proportional representation. 'We took them to the cleaners!' concluded one of the Prime Minister's aides.[38] For his part, Steel could argue that during the lifetime of the pact over the next eighteen months, the Liberals acted as a moderating force and prevented any 'further expansion of socialism'. Voters were not greatly impressed by the new arrangement; both parties lost ground at local elections in the spring of 1977. Nevertheless, having successfully bought time, Callaghan was relying on economic recovery to win back sceptical voters. This second element in the government's revival came about with surprising rapidity. The IMF loan succeeded in calming the foreign exchanges, and with the world recession finally coming to an end, Britain's economic indicators began to look more favourable. Union adherence to a ten per cent ceiling on pay rises helped to bring inflation down to single figures, sterling showed a strong recovery, and the balance of payments moved into surplus. The Chancellor never had to draw more than half the stand-by credits available, and much earlier than anticipated he was able to celebrate 'Sod off Day' – the moment when he became free of IMF control.[39]

Healey still had his critics. Economic experts noted that the main features of Britain's 'industrial disease' remained untouched. Within the Labour movement, a young Tribunite MP, Neil Kinnock, expressed a common view that ministers were treating 'the City of London as if it were some kind of winnable Tory marginal' by cutting spending on education, health and social security.[40] Over the past decade many constituency parties were in the process of being transformed by a 'new "bed-sit brigade" of youthful, far-left, middle-class zealots'. This was most noticeable in inner-city areas with shrinking memberships; though the decline in numbers was slower than in the late 1960s, the party was still losing an average of 11,000 members each year.[41] These new activists were less deferential than their more working-class predecessors in the era of Attlee and Gaitskell, and openly worked – through groups such as the Campaign for Labour Party Democracy (CLPD), founded in 1973 – to make the leadership more accountable to the rank-and-file. Only in this way, it was argued, would it be possible to avoid 'betrayals' of socialism such as the IMF cuts. The trauma of the IMF episode, and the attendant abandonment by Labour ministers of the traditional goal of full employment, provided a further spur to the growth of radical opinion. By 1978, the constituency section of the NEC no longer contained any supporters of the party leadership, and Callaghan was continually receiving a rough ride. But for the time being the real concern of Labour's 'new left' was with organisational change. In the words of Paul Whiteley: 'The disillusionment with the 1964–70 government had led to a reformulation of Labour's policy goals in a more radical socialist direction. When this proved insufficient to change party policies after 1974, attention was focused on internal party democracy.'[42] After a controversial move by local activists to remove a right-wing minister, Reg Prentice, particular attention focused on selection procedures. At the 1978 conference, an attempt to introduce mandatory reselection of MPs was voted down, but there was every indication that the sponsors of the motion would continue their battle.[43] Pressure for greater accountability, it now seemed, could only be resisted by the leadership if it was able to demonstrate public satisfaction with an unreformed Labour party.

By mid-1978 sustained economic recovery did look set to produce political dividends. Mrs Thatcher's lead in the opinion polls had been whittled away, and press speculation began to focus on the possibility of an autumn general election. The Prime Minister was tempted to exploit the opportunity, as he saw it, of depicting himself 'as the leader of a left wing party heading towards the centre while she [Mrs Thatcher] is the leader of a right-wing party heading towards the right'.[44] There were still several clouds on the horizon, not least the perennial 'union problem'. Thinking aloud in a radio interview, Callaghan had been tempted into the suggestion that wage rises might be restricted to five per cent by 1979. When this figure hardened into government policy, many union leaders reacted with disbelief, recognising that the average worker's reduction in purchasing power since 1975 already represented – in the words of one Whitehall official – 'the most severe cut in real wages for twenty years'.[45] The cabinet nevertheless approved a five per cent limit on pay deals in the summer; ministers calculated that an election, which many privately urged on the Prime Minister, was certain to come before the autumn pay round got under way. After lengthy consultations, however, Callaghan decided not to risk an appeal to the country. He was ultimately persuaded by party officials that Labour's position in the marginal constituencies, though it had recovered since 1976, was not strong enough to deliver a parliamentary majority. A few more months of economic growth and wage restraint, he figured, was more likely to produce a solid victory in the spring of 1979.[46] At the TUC conference the Prime Minister announced his decision by teasing those who had been expecting an election with an old music hall song: 'There was I, waiting at the church'. With hindsight, this single decision was to have fatal consequences: far from delivering victory, it helped to consign Labour to the electoral wilderness.

Party workers and union leaders alike felt let down by 'Jim's little joke'. Instead of being pre-election window dressing, the government's wage norm was to be a reality over the winter. After three years of pay restraint and depressed living standards, this was too much to bear. 'You can only stretch an elastic band so far', argued one delegate as the Labour conference in October voted overwhelmingly to return to free collective bargaining. After the TUC's General Council took a similar view, the green light was given for member unions to begin negotiating higher settlements. In December Ford motor workers were awarded a fifteen per cent pay increase following a protracted strike. Thereafter the flood gates opened, as various groups of low-paid workers, mostly in public service unions, aggressively pursued their wage claims.

What followed in the early months of 1979 was to be long remembered as the 'winter of discontent':

> Strikes hit the National Health Service and operations had to be cancelled. Tanker drivers stopped deliveries, causing petrol shortages. . . . Garbage piled up in the streets as the result of a stoppage by local authority workers; newspapers carried pictures of rats amid the rubbish in Piccadily Circus. Even some gravediggers downed tools, leaving the dead unburied; pickets turned away funeral corteges from cemetary gates.[47]

Callaghan initially tried to play down the significance of these events. The phrase 'Crisis. What crisis?' was repeatedly hung round his neck by a hostile press, although he never uttered these precise words. Indeed as industrial stoppages rose higher than at any time since the General Strike of 1926, he increasingly condemned 'free collective vandalism'.[48] By the time ministers conceded wage increases of ten per cent to end the unrest in March, the damage had been done. Labour's anti-inflation strategy lay in ruins, the party's claim that it alone could work harmoniously with the unions was destroyed, and the Conservatives had surged ahead in the opinion polls. With all the opposition forces united in anger – including Nationalist MPs dismayed by the failure to introduce devolution for Scotland and Wales – the government was narrowly beaten on a 'no confidence' motion in the Commons, thus giving Callaghan the dubious distinction of being the first Prime Minister since Ramsay MacDonald to be defeated in such a way. He duly resigned and announced that the election would be held on 3 May.

The events of the past few months inevitably allowed the Conservatives to go into the campaign on the offensive. With the support of much of the press, Mrs Thatcher hit upon a populist message – that the time was ripe to break with a Labour Britain that had resulted in overmighty trade unions and government spending out of control. Instead, the Tories promised, as in 1970, to restore the balance between the individual and the state. This would be done in several ways: by conquering inflation through tight monetary control; by curbing union power with new laws on balloting and picketing; by promoting private enterprise through lower taxation and privatisation; and by widening home ownership through the sale of council houses. By contrast, Callaghan – rather like Wilson in 1970 – opted for safety first. He emphasised the twin themes of competence, arguing that recession had given way to controlled recovery, and conciliation, promising to implement a new concordat with the unions.[49] Commentators were agreed that the Prime Minister made an impressive personal showing in seeking to exploit the untried radicalism of his opponent. But the 'winter of discontent' had done nothing for the image of the party or for the idea of conciliation as the best way forward. The outcome was a swing to the Conservatives of 5.1 per cent, the largest at any election since the war, and more than enough to provide Mrs Thatcher with a comfortable majority. Regional variations, such as a net swing to Labour in Scotland, provided only a crumb of comfort. In the Midlands, London and the South-East, there were massive defections from Labour, especially among women, skilled workers and new voters.[50] There could be no disguising the crushing nature of the defeat. The party's share of the total poll, at 36.9 per cent, was its lowest since the disastrous showing of 1931. The electorate had delivered its verdict on five years of Labour government.

V

The election defeat casts a long shadow over judgements about Labour in the 1970s. The 1974 government stands condemned both for economic mismanagement and for failing to prevent fragmentation in party ranks. As a result, Wilson and Callaghan have tended to be portrayed 'as a pair of shabby pragmatists, waiting for something to turn up, the Estragon and Vladimir of degenerate Labourism'.[51] Several cautionary notes might be sounded. Both leaders, as we have seen, had to face the acute difficulties of inherited inflation and world recession, which together made for a more hostile environment than encountered by any post-war government. Nor was the record of the 1974–79 quite so dismal as its detractors make out. The centre-right's loyalty to the leadership was based upon a conviction that, whatever pain came with deflation, a Labour administration was better than the alternative of untrammelled Conservatism. In social policy, the record may not have matched that of the 1960s, but it did produce worthwhile reforms such as the continued spread of comprehensive schools, equal opportunities legislation and a new Commission for Racial Equality. Similarly, Labour loyalists could take comfort that if the defeat of inflation necessitated cash limits and tighter monetary control, it did not require the type of penal action against trade unions advocated by Mrs Thatcher. Recent studies have borne out the need for a more balanced appraisal of the economic record:

> Despite a large-scale and in some ways innovative incomes policy experiment, the government did not move closer to solving the country's enduring inflation/unemployment problem and it failed to accelerate the underlying growth of the economy; but it was not unique among British governments before, or since, in these respects. What it did was to move pragmatically to adapt policy to the new environment of higher inflation and slower growth. Given this achievement it seems fair to claim that the Labour governments left the economy and the policy-making machinery in better condition in 1979 than they found them in 1974.[52]

Callaghan's reputation would certainly stand much higher had he gone to the country six months earlier, with inflation in single figures and disposable incomes rising. Fatally of course he chose otherwise, and in the interim his wage restraint 'task force' – unlike Mrs Thatcher's three years later – sank without trace. This inevitably overshadowed much of what had gone before: for if the economy was in no worse shape by 1979, the same could not be said of the party. Callaghan's premiership had left Labour facing the abyss.

The 1979 election had seen the most decisive rejection of Labour for nearly half a century. The party had been decimated as an electoral force in large parts of the country: throughout southern England outside London, in rural areas, and in many small towns, with the exception of mining districts. Labour had been hardest hit, moreover, in its own natural constituency, with swings well above the national average among younger and skilled workers – many of them trade unionists – in areas such as the car industry suburbs, the Lancashire coalfields and the new towns.[53] Inquests into the defeat inevitably focused on the early months of 1979; Callaghan himself interpreted the outcome as a 'vote against the events of last winter'. But survey evidence indicated that this told only part of the story, and that much of the damage had been done by the government's record over a longer period. Unemployment at its highest level for forty years and a prolonged squeeze on pay while prices were escalating: these had been the root cause of disaffection for many working-class voters. The end result was not simply the product of material ambition inexorably eroding the Labour vote. Notwithstanding the intensity of Britain's economic difficulties in the 1970s, which made some degree of disenchantment unavoidable, the party had clearly contributed to its own demise. From the leadership down there were few real efforts to keep pace with Mrs Thatcher in constructing a new populist agenda. By contrast, Labour was losing touch with the aspiring classes of Britain's 'property owning democracy'. Many aspects of government policy such as high taxation and further nationalisation – often cherished by the enthusiasts who dominated shrunken inner-city Labour parties – had become deeply unpopular with the broader electorate. By clinging to past shibboleths, reflected one MP, Labour had become indelibly associated in the public mind with nothing more than 'slums, decaying shipyards, immigrants, cloth caps and caring . . . for minorities and underdogs'.[54] The significance of one election can of course be exaggerated; the Tories had promised a counter-revolution in 1970 and yet were out of office within four years. But if Labour was to recover lost ground, then it had to do so from a lower base than ever before, and it had to do so at a time when the old link between social class and voting intention was visibly crumbling.[55]

If unity was a pre-requisite for staging a fightback, the signs did not look good in the summer of 1979. For months after the election, Labour activists became embroiled in acrimonious exchanges about the causes of defeat, with particular attention focusing on the role of the unions. From 1970 onwards Harold Wilson had been determined that there should be no repeat of *In Place of Strife*; that Labour would base its appeal on its unique ability to work with the unions. This applied equally to Callaghan: 'The Keeper of the Cloth Cap' as he had been dubbed after resisting Barbara Castle's proposals for reform in 1970. For many ministers, the winter of discontent was a strange way of repaying the legal benefits conferred on the union movement since 1974, and there was no doubting who was to blame for putting Mrs Thatcher into power. According to Denis Healey: 'The cowardice and irresponsibility of some union leaders in abdicating responsibility at this time guaranteed her election; it left them with no grounds for complaining about her subsequent action against them.'[56] For their part, union leaders complained that the Prime Minister was guilty of trying to impose an unrealistic wage policy. The Labour left went further. 'Those who follow Mr Callaghan's line of argument, in seeking to explain the present disaster in terms of union intransigence', wrote Ken Coates, 'should rather bend their . . . powers to the task of explaining what it was that transformed the social contracting trade union saints of 1975, 6, 7 and part of 1978 into the demonic fiends about whom we read in the *Daily Mail* of last winter'.[57] The government, in other words, had been destroyed by its own actions: by pushing trade unionists too far, by the spending cuts of 'Denis the thug', as he was known in the pages of Tony Benn's diary, and by failing to deliver on manifesto commitments such as a wealth tax and devolution for Scotland.[58] Claims that the party would have won on an overtly socialist programme, as in 1974, were met with the counter charge that 'left-wing extremism' was guilty of putting off thousands of potential Labour voters.

The recriminations that took place after May 1979 were symptomatic of a deeper identity crisis. The question that Wilson had evaded in the 1960s still remained to be answered: what precisely was the role of Labour in a modern capitalist society? Revisionists within the party, who had hitherto led the efforts to come up with an answer, had clearly declined in influence, especially as the centre-right had lost some of its most able lieutenants. Disillusioned with Labour politics, Roy Jenkins had departed to take up the presidency of the European Commission –

a loss that was greeted with rejoicing by his opponents. 'Will you be voting for Roy Jenkins?', one of his supporters is reported to have asked during the 1976 leadership contest. 'No lad', came the reply from an elderly MP, 'we're all Labour here'.[59] By the time of Crosland's death in 1977, the old revisionist notion of achieving equality via economic growth and redistributive taxation had been thoroughly discredited. This did not mean that the Labour left were able to dictate policy-making. In spite of increased militancy among the rank-and-file, the organised pressure groups of the new left contained only a few thousand members. Domination of the NEC was not enough to prevent Healey's spending cuts or to influence the leader's preferred programme, as Tribunite MPs found to their disgust when proposals for a hard-hitting manifesto in 1979 were sidelined. In effect, Labour in the 1970s had become 'all but doctrineless'.[60] In place of Attlee's corporate socialism, Gaitskell's revisionism and Wilson's scientific planning, Callaghan could offer only an old-style Labourism that had manifestly gone out of fashion. When this was made brutally apparent at the 1979 election, a resumption of 'civil war' for the ideological heart of the party became unavoidable. 'To pretend in this situation that socialists and social democrats are all part of the same great Movement', wrote one disenchanted, former MP David Marquand, in July 1979, 'is to live a lie. But it is a lie the Labour Party has to live if it is to live at all'.[61] During the next eighteen months it became clear that socialists and social democrats could no longer live together; whether the party would 'live at all' remained to be seen.

5

THE END OF THE ROAD?, 1979–92

I

In the decade that followed the election defeat of 1979, it was widely assumed that Jim Callaghan would be the last Labour Prime Minister. Mrs Thatcher's economic record during her first adminstration was far from impressive. Her promised assault on Britain's post-war settlement, with its attempt to shake off state collectivism and replace it with an 'enterprise culture', was overshadowed by a fresh recession. Two years into office unemployment was rising steadily towards three million – a figure that would have been unthinkable a decade earlier. This, together with tough penal legislation, finally helped to quell the trade union militancy of recent years, but it also led to a sharp fall in manufacturing output, with the north of England most severely hit. And yet in 1983 the Conservatives were returned to power with the second-largest majorty of seats since the war. As all the frustrations of the Wilson-Callaghan era came to the surface, Labour had destroyed any prospect it had of regaining power by engaging in protracted blood-letting. The party fared even more abysmally in 1983, on a platform reflecting the increased assertiveness of the left, than it had done in 1979. So dismal was Labour's performance that it was seriously challenged for second place by a nascent 'centre force', the Liberal-Social Democratic Alliance, which made the best third party showing since the 1920s. Friends and enemies alike spoke of Labour being in a state of terminal decline, racked by internal dissent and incapable of adjusting to changing social realities. In the event, rumours of the party's death were exaggerated. Under the leadership of Neil Kinnock, a partial recovery took place in the mid-1980s. The so-called 'hard left' was marginalised and strenuous efforts were made to bring the party back into the mainstream of European social democracy. Low inflation and resumed economic growth were sufficient to carry Mrs Thatcher into the record books with a third successive election victory in 1987, this time with Labour in a clear but distant second place. If nothing else, Kinnock's party was still in business.

By the late 1980s there were signs that Labour's painful rehabilitation was nearing completion. Mrs Thatcher's 'economic miracle', if it ever existed at all, turned out to be short-lived; her bold claims about the success of the free market confounded by a mixture of policy errors and deteriorating world conditions after 1987. Survey evidence suggested that voters had not been entirely won over to Thatcherite values, and Labour began to build up the type of sustained lead in the polls that it had not enjoyed since the dying days of the Macmillan regime. With the Alliance disintegrating, the party swept to victory in the European elections of 1989 – its first major success at the polling booths for fifteen years. Perhaps Callaghan would after all pass on his mantle to Neil Kinnock. Not even the dramatic downfall of Margaret Thatcher – removed by her own party as it contemplated electoral defeat – could dent Labour's renewed optimism. Her emollient successor John Major managed to undo the most unpopular legacies of Thatcherism, notably the poll tax, but he was powerless to prevent the second recession of the 1980s dragging on to become the longest since the 1930s. After thirteen years in power, the Conservatives were apparently no closer to tackling Britain's economic malaise, and to an unprecedented extent it was the Tory heartlands of southern England that were bearing the brunt of rising bankruptcies and job losses. In spite of all this, the Conservatives triumphed again at the 1992 general election. Labour was not only defeated for the fourth time in a row, but it failed to make up sufficient ground to suggest that 'one more push' might carry it back to power. The role of permanent opposition beckoned. Why then was the party able to survive against the odds and yet fall well short of breaking the Tory stranglehold at Westminster? How should we explain the paradox of 'resilient but enfeebled Labourism'?[1]

II

Labour's response to defeat in 1979 was to press the self-destruct button. In the words of one former minister: 'Within weeks of the coming to power of the most virulently right-wing, class-orientated government that we've had in Britain since before the war, [Labour] was assaulting itself and continuing to rake over the alleged failures of the previous periods . . . tearing itself apart in the frantic search for scapegoats.'[2] Callaghan's defeat gave greater credence to the familiar cry of the party's new left: that Labour had alienated voters by betraying its socialist principles. This argument was used by rank-and-file activists to intensify their campaign for organisational reform, which had been gathering pace during the late 1970s. The threat posed by the new left, or 'polytariat' as it was dubbed, provoked a belated response from the centre-right. In 1977 the Campaign for Labour Victory had been established in an effort to rally moderate opinion, but with limited success. Its failure, according to one member, was threefold: 'it was London based, a leadership organisation . . . had the Common Market obsession which . . . is not the basis of a socialist programme and . . . also had a lot of personality problems.'[3] Electoral defeat put further pressure on the Labour right. After losing ground throughout the 1970s, its task was now made more difficult by the need to defend a discredited government. The annual conference at Brighton in 1979 gave a clear indication of the way the wind was blowing. Jim Callaghan came in for some harsh criticism, notably from a candidate defeated at the polls, who reflected his local party's anger about the watering down of socialist policies: '"Jim will fix it," they said. Ay, he fixed it. He fixed all of us.'[4] The conference went on to vote for the introduction of mandatory reselection of MPs – the first major victory for the left in its struggle to secure greater accountablilty.

Over the following year, the battle between left and right intensified. In some respects, Labour was following a similar pattern to the early 1970s: then too there had been in-fighting over the changes required to recover lost electoral ground. But a decade later there were some crucial differences. Several of the major unions no longer displayed instinctive loyalty to the leadership, and after 1979 the left had a spokesman, in Tony Benn, who was capable of securing broad support for policy changes. He was also – by virtue of his compelling oratory and televisual skills – a natural leader for disaffected constituency activists, themselves posing a more cohesive challenge than hitherto. In 1980 the Rank and File Mobilising Committee was set up as an umbrella organisation embracing all those seeking fundamental change. This included – following the relaxation of rules on proscribed organisations – several Trotskyist groups, notably Militant Tendency, a 'party within the party but disguised as a periodical'.[5] Confronted with 'Bennery' at Westminster and 'entryism' in the localities, the Labour right proved unable and unwilling to mount a counter-attack. There were signs that some former ministers might instead 'jump ship'. David Owen, as Foreign Secretary for the last two years of Callaghan's administration, was particularly dismayed by moves to introduce a non nuclear defence policy, and in August 1980 he joined with Shirley Williams and Bill Rodgers – the 'Gang of Three' – to warn that a new party of 'conscience and reform' might become necessary in the near future.[6] Such a possibility came closer at the annual conference in Blackpool, where the mood was set by Tony Benn on the first day. To rapturous applause, he declared that the next Labour government would, within a matter of weeks, abolish the House of Lords, extend public ownership and leave the European Community. Benn's ideas, together with unilateral nuclear disarmament, were enthusiastically adopted as party policy. 'For the Gang of Three, in urgent and much-photographed conclave on the conference floor, these votes seemed like a deportation order.'[7]

Jim Callaghan's response to this turn of events was to resign. He did so not simply because his appeals for unity had been scorned, but also because he hoped to influence the succession. The annual conference agreed in principle to a further demand from the left – that the party leader be chosen by an 'electoral college' rather than by the PLP – but details of the new scheme remained to be worked out at a special conference scheduled for January 1981. By resigning sooner rather than later, Callaghan hoped that a final contest under the old rules would ensure victory for Denis Healey, the candidate best equipped to continue the fight against the left. At first it looked as though there would be little opposition to Healey, 'a leader of standing, intellect and, as he modestly kept telling people, world reputation'.[8] Tony Benn was persuaded by his supporters that, pending the introduction of the new electoral college for which the left had fought, he should not stand in an 'illegitimate' election. As a result, considerable pressure was put on Michael Foot to stand as a candidate for the left. Rather to his surprise, Foot defeated Healey by 139 votes to 129 on a second ballot. There were several reasons why MPs rejected the candidate preferred by four out of five voters, and chose instead a sixty-seven year old presented by the press over the years as a 'long-haired Marxist extremist'. On the Labour left, there was considerable 'stop Healey' sentiment among those who could not forgive his record as Chancellor in the 1970s; some cynically believed Foot could act as a caretaker until Benn could assume the leadership. Many though voted for Michael Foot for more positive reasons. He was believed to be much better equipped than Healey to maintain unity, and his Bevanite past meant he more accurately represented the party's desire for radical change after the alleged failings of the Wilson-Callaghan government. In short, he was respected as Labour's 'favourite figurehead, the angry old man of the left, the man who carried the Ark of its socialist covenant'.[9] Nevertheless, the outcome may ultimately have been decided by 'sabotage': several MPs on the right did not deny that they had voted for Foot in order to justify leaving the party.[10] Their departure was not long delayed.

The occasion for a major split in Labour ranks was the Wembley conference of January 1981, which proved to be Foot's first humiliation as party leader. His own preferred option for the new electoral college was that there should be a 50:25:25 balance between the PLP, the unions and constituency parties in electing future leaders. But the Labour left believed this would perpetuate the dominance of the centre-right, and after a series of byzantine manoeuvres, managed to carry a 40:30:30 system, with the trade unions possessing the major share of votes. One of the organisers of the Campaign for Labour Party Democracy claimed this as the greatest triumph yet of the new left – a victory over 'the National Executive Committee, the Transport and General Workers' Union, the Parliamentary Party and Michael Foot. We won against all the establishment figures'.[11] Foot's misery was compounded when his appeals for unity were brushed aside by the 'Gang of Three'. Using the rejection of the principle of 'one member, one vote' as a pretext – though they had never previously advocated such a system – Owen, Williams and Rodgers joined with Roy Jenkins amidst a blaze of media attention to form the Social Democratic Party (SDP). Within months, the new party could claim over twenty MPs, most of them defectors from Labour ranks, and had formed a new 'Alliance' with the Liberals which aimed to 'break the mould' by occupying the centre ground of British politics. In spite of this obvious threat to its future existence, the Labour party responded with a renewed bout of blood-letting. Tony Benn, ignoring pleas from Foot that unity was essential, decided to test the new electoral college arrangements by challenging Denis Healey for the Deputy Leadership. Thus over the summer of 1981 voters were treated to the spectacle of a bitter personal contest, marked by regular shouting down of Healey's speeches and by vitriolic attacks on Benn from the emerging 'soft left' for his 'divisive tactics'. After the incumbent retained his post by the narrowest of margins, one MP concluded that this might at least mark a turning point in the internal power struggle: 'Denis Healey', he optimistically claimed, 'has saved the Labour Party'.[12]

By 1982 the party was looking more and more as if it needed saving. Despite its internal difficulties, Labour had remained ahead of the Conservatives in the opinion polls for most of the past year. In the midst of a deep recession, with unemployment soaring and bankruptcies mounting, Mrs Thatcher was rated as the most unpopular Prime Minister in living memory. Her fortunes were unexpectedly transformed by the Falklands war, the successful outcome of which left the Tories with a substantial lead in the polls. From this moment on, Mrs Thatcher's fighting qualities and 'resolute approach' were increasingly contrasted with the alleged shortcomings of the Labour leader. 'One by one', notes Robert Harris, 'Foot's assets seemed to turn into liabilities. His kindness looked like weakness; his tolerance, indecision; his culture, bookishness; his originality, eccentricity; his sense of history, the obsessions of an old man living in the past'.[13] In some respects Foot, backed by union leaders alarmed at the hostility of Tory ministers, did manage to initiate a fightback by moderates against the 'hard left'. Proposals for NEC control over the manifesto were defeated, and it was Foot who began moves to expel members of the Militant Tendency from the party.[14] But Labour's association with 'extremism' would not go away. Efforts by several left wing local authorities to break with the past by introducing 'grass-roots socialism', giving priority to issues such as sexual and racial equality, were pilloried by the tabloid press, which set out to find 'Britain's barmiest council'.[15] Attempts to oust Militant dragged on in full public gaze, and the damage caused by the 'loony left' tag was thrown into sharp relief at the Bermondsey by-election early in 1983. Local party workers insisted on adopting Peter Tatchell, a candidate Foot had once said he would never endorse because of his views on extra-parliamentary action. After a vicious campaign in which Tatchell was vilified by the press as an Australian draft-dodging homosexual, Labour's vote fell by 38 per cent and the seat was lost to the Alliance. Many MPs now believed that Foot should resign before things got worse. Pressure on his leadership subsided after Labour narrowly won the Darlington by-election a few weeks later, though few were persuaded that Foot could carry the party to victory in any forthcoming election. This view was shared by Labour's own private polling research, which concluded that 'the overall image was of a party on the decline, which was currently implausible as an alternative government.'[16]

Mrs Thatcher therefore went into the election of June 1983 in a far stronger position than could have been imagined two years earlier. With inflation falling and recession blamed on 'world conditions', she was able to launch a slick campaign promising more of the same if re-elected: firm control of public spending, tax cuts, privatisation and trade union reform. By contrast, neither of the opposition parties mounted an effective challenge. Whereas the Alliance struggled to establish a clear image, both in terms of policy and leadership, Labour found that its identity was distinct but disliked. The party's programme was subjected to a relentless assault by press advocates of a Tory victory, now read by three out of four newspaper readers. Two elements of the lengthy manifesto – dubbed 'the longest suicide note in history' – came under particularly intense scrutiny. On the economy, Labour's pledge to cut unemployment from three to one million within five years was rubbished on the grounds that any expansionary programme would lead to renewed inflation, especially as there was no formal wages agreement with the unions. It was also claimed that Labour's promise to take Britain out of the EEC would cost far more jobs than would be created. The second issue focused on by the Tory tabloids was Labour's contradictory non-nuclear defence policy, which promised to cancel Trident while including Polaris in disarmament negotiations. With opinion polls suggesting that less than twenty per cent of voters favoured unilateralism, this approach was ridiculed along the lines that Britain would be left defenceless. Unlike previous Labour leaders, Michael Foot did not attempt to run away from manifesto commitments, though his example was not followed by other party luminaries such as Jim Callaghan, who repaid Foot's loyalty during his own premiership by publicly denouncing unilateral disarmament. Callaghan's intervention was indicative an increasingly shambolic campaign, with Foot himself being mercilessly characterised as a dishevelled, disorganised figure unfit for high office. On 26 May, amidst rumours that the leader was being urged by colleagues to stand down, the party's General Secretary, Jim Mortimer, was forced to take the unusual step of reaffirming that Foot was still in charge.[17]

Events during the last week suggested that far from narrowing the Conservative lead, Labour was slipping at the expense of the Alliance. This trend was confirmed when the results showed that Labour had suffered its most crushing defeat in post-war politics, far worse than 1979. The party's share of the total vote collapsed to 27.6

per cent, only 2 per cent ahead of the Alliance. With a parliamentary majority of 144, Mrs Thatcher had secured, symbolically, a 1945 in reverse. Although Labour's vote held up reasonably in areas hardest hit by the recession, the party was decimated in southern England, much of which had continued to prosper. In the whole of this area, Labour held only three seats outside inner London, and because of the Alliance challenge came second in only eighteen of the remaining 150 constituencies. Members of the skilled working-class, the 'C2s' who often worked in the private sector and were taking the opportunity to buy their council properties, turned away from Labour in droves. As one despairing MP concluded: 'A once great party, a party which formed the government for half the post-war period up to 1979, was reduced to a rump.'[18] There was little dispute amongst commentators that this was a verdict on the whole drift of events since 1979. Michael Foot, who resigned in the immediate aftermath of defeat, provided a convenient scapegoat, though many recognised that his failings only exacerbated the scale of a defeat made inevitable by deep divisions and by a programme that aroused profound distrust on the doorstep. One survey revealed that nearly half of Conservative voters explained their preference in terms of a fear of letting Labour in, a higher proportion than those expressing a positive desire to see a Tory government.[19] Nor was there much dispute among pundits about the main consequences of the election. In the first place, it paved the way for the consolidation of Mrs Thatcher's mission to create an enterprise economy. And secondly, it raised the question of who constituted the real opposition to the Conservatives. The Alliance may not have 'broken the mould', but by achieving the best third party result for sixty years it could still harbour thoughts of supplanting Labour as the centre-left alternative in British politics. As its critics were not slow to point out, the Labour party was on the verge of going out of business.

III

The sceptics were to be confounded during the course of Mrs Thatcher's second term, though it was a close run thing. In part

Labour survived because the Alliance proved unable to deliver a knock-out punch. Despite further by-election gains, the Alliance struggled to establish an identity that would attract large numbers of voters; this problem was compounded by the refusal of the SDP's new leader, David Owen, to contemplate merger with the Liberals. Much of the credit for Labour's survival, however, rested with the determination of its own new leader. Neither of the contenders for the deputy's post in 1981 put themeselves forward after Michael Foot's resignation. Denis Healey ruled himself out as being too old, and Tony Benn was ineligible having lost his Bristol East seat at the election. The leadership was thus contested between two members of a younger political generation. Roy Hattersley sought to rally support on the centre-right of the party by building on some of the Croslandite themes of the 1970s, such as caution on public ownership. He also injected life into proceedings by attacking Michael Foot, a move described by his opponents as 'a bit like hitting your own granny'.[20] To criticise a figure still revered by the party faithful was interpreted as a sign of desperation. From the outset, it was clear that Hattersley would be unable to prevent his rival, Neil Kinnock, from sweeping to victory. Kinnock's popularity was based on various factors: his working-class origins as the son of a Welsh miner, his forceful and outgoing personality, and above all his left-wing credentials. As a young MP in the 1970s, he had been an articulate critic of the discredited Wilson-Callaghan regime, and in the early 1980s he emerged as a champion of the soft left, scornful of 'Bennery' and crucially refusing to vote for Benn in the contest against Healey. Hence Kinnock became at 41 Labour's youngest-ever leader by capturing 71 per cent of the electoral college vote, though Hattersley gained sufficient support to help him secure the deputy's post.[21] This 'dream ticket' leadership recognised that Labour had an electoral mountain to climb. Aside from the Alliance threat, the party was faced with a government that could remain in power even if deserted by one in four of its 1983 supporters. If he was to get any further than the foothills, Kinnock first had to reunite and assert control over his own forces.

His chosen strategy for moving the party forward was to marginalise those whom he felt were 'so obsessed with ideology that they cannot see the people for the slogans'.[22] This task was made easier by the blame attached to hard left extremism for the 1983 defeat and by the loss of momentum amongst groups that flourished in the 1970s. Kinnock's level of support in the leadership contest, under rules favoured by the hard left, also put him in a strong position to deal with his opponents. He was thus able to distance himself from the miners' leader, Arthur Scargill, during the national strike of 1984–85, and he made a hard-hitting attack at the 1985 conference on the 'grotesque chaos' of Labour councillors in Liverpool hiring taxis to deliver redundancy notices to their own workers. He also continued the process of implicitly reviving the proscribed list by moving to expel members of Militant Tendency. This culminated in the expulsion of leading Liverpool 'Militants', such as Derek Hatton, during the summer of 1986; a move supported by mainstream party opinion to an extent that would have been unimagineable a few years earlier.[23] By this time, Kinnock had built up a strong power base on the centre-left. He did so by promoting those whom he felt belonged to the 'radical, but realistic left', including several union leaders thrown on the defensive by reforms such as the banning of secondary industrial action and anxious to find ways of countering the decline in union membership – falling since 1980 by some 500,000 every year.[24] With such support Kinnock, unlike Callaghan or Wilson from the mid-1970s, was able to demonstrate his managerial control of the party by dominating the NEC.[25] Nor did he shrink from the task of internal modernisation. An attempt in 1984 to extend party democracy, by introducing the one member, one vote principle in the selection of parliamentary candidates, foundered on union opposition, but efforts to overhaul Labour's organisational structure met with greater success. The appointment of Herbert Morrison's grandson, Peter Mandelson, as publicity director meant that henceforth the party sought to look outwards once more towards the public, rather than appearing preoccupied with its own internal concerns.

One of Mandelson's tasks was to convince voters that Labour had the policies to deal with the problems of the 1980s. 'If we want to win', Kinnock said shortly after becoming leader, 'we have to commend the common sense of socialism'. Over the next three years, the programme that had proved so unattractive in 1983 was gradually modified, and new ways were sought of appealing to those 'whose upward mobility, increased expectations and extended horizons are largely the result of opportunities afforded by our movement in the past'.[26] Opposition to the sale of council houses was dropped, and pledges were made to retain at least some of Mrs Thatcher's trade union laws, while adding a 'Workers' Charter' to protect employees. The central economic demand of the Labour left since the war – increased state intervention in the economy – was sidelined as nationalisation gave way to the more limited concept of 'social ownership'. Attempts were also made to build on techniques used by successful economies overseas. Manufacturing industry, which had been hard hit by the recession of 1979–81, was to be revived with the assistance of a National Investment Bank based on the Japanese model; while western European practice was the inspiration for Labour's plan to improve technical training and to hold annual tripartite summits between employers, unions and government. The party also reconciled itself – after twenty years of agonising – to continued British membership of the European Community, though there was less movement on defence policy. Kinnock emphasised his commitment to NATO in order to demonstrate that he was no isolationist, but party sentiment remained firmly behind the cancellation of the Trident programme and the renunciation of nuclear weapons on British soil. Nevertheless, by late 1985 *The Times* could describe Labour's new programme as 'Gaitskellism from the left of centre'.[27] Although Kinnock himself may not have welcomed such a definition, it pointed to a remarkable transformation. Within three years, he had managed to jettison Bennite-style British socialism and replaced it with a variation on European social democracy.

Kinnock's commitment to organisational and policy change made some impression on the voting public. For much of Mrs Thatcher's second term, Labour seemed capable of not only fending off the Alliance, but actually mounting a serious challenge to the Conservatives. In spite of personal abuse from the Tory tabloids, who depicted him as an inexperienced lightweight, Kinnock was able to take comfort from a sharp rise in Labour's opinion poll rating for several months after assuming the leadership. Any further progress was checked by the lenghty miners' strike, during which party leaders were torn between sympathy for workers threatened with pit closures and reluctance to condone the unpopular picketing methods associated with Arthur Scargill.[28] But by the summer of 1985, with unemployment still rising, Labour was again edging ahead in the polls – a position confirmed by Kinnock's combative attack on Militant at the Bournemouth conference and by the Prime Minister's embarrassment over the 'Westland affair'. In April 1986 the party secured its first by-election gain for several years, at Fulham, and followed this up with encouraging local election results. Mandelson and his team redoubled their efforts to sell Labour's remodelled image. The red rose replaced the red flag as the party's emblem, and glossy new policy packages – combining a traditional concern for social justice with promises of increased individual choice – were launched amidst much media attention. As delegates gathered for the annual conference at Blackpool in October 1986, the party's image makers hoped to set the tone for what might be an election year by focusing on the pernicious social consequences of Thatcherism. But in practice, Blackpool served to highlight the shallowness of Labour's recovery. As the skeletons from the early 1980s began to come out of the cupboard, any serious prospect of winning a forthcoming election rapidly receded.

As in 1983, defence did much of the damage. The vote in favour of non nuclear defence at the Liberal assembly in September 1986 not only upset David Owen and highlighted Alliance divisions. It also meant that the whole conference season would be dominated by 'the bomb', with Conservative ministers again taking every opportunity to lambast Labour's unilateral stance. Neil Kinnock's CND past made this area of policy largely exempt from reappraisal. In spite of efforts to argue that savings from the elimination of nuclear weapons would be channelled into improving conventional forces, Labour's lead in the polls disappeared overnight. The trend of a swing back towards the government was reinforced by economic recovery and by Kinnock's humiliation at the hands of President Reagan, who made no secret of the US government's preference for Mrs Thatcher's style of politics. The sight of the Labour leader being treated dismissively in

Washington allowed the Tory tabloids to step up their personal attacks on Kinnock: not only was he a 'Welsh windbag', he was also inconsequential on the world stage.[29] In addition, the press found another effective means of undermining Labour's credibility. Over the winter of 1986–87, there was a sustained effort to demonstrate that, in spite of superficial appearances, the 'loony left' was alive and well. The climax came with the Greenwich by-election of February 1987, occasioned by the death of the sitting Labour MP. To the dismay of party leaders, local activists chose as their candidate Deidre Wood, a known supporter of some of the more controversial activities of left-wing Labour councils. Although effective as a doorstep campaigner, Wood was viciously ridiculed by the tabloids, who helped to build up a bandwagon effect that carried the SDP's Rosie Barnes to victory. For Neil Kinnock, this piece of bad luck was the equivalent of the Bermondsey by-election in 1983. As the Alliance crept back into second place in the polls, it looked as though Kinnock's efforts at reforming the party would come to nothing. Greenwich, together with local election results that confirmed a Tory resurgence, provided the backcloth to Mrs Thatcher's attempt in June 1987 to secure a third general election victory.

Labour's campaign set out to ensure that the shambles of 1983 would not be repeated. The manifesto was pointedly kept short and sharply focused, with the main emphasis on a jobs and anti-poverty programme to be implemented in the first two years of power. There was also much firmer central control of the campaign than in 1983. At the party's headquarters in Walworth Road, Campaign Co-ordinator Bryan Gould was constantly on hand to maintain contact with key marginal seats and to focus media attention on Labour's traditionally strong 'caring issues' of health and education. Even further removed from the experience of 1983 was the party's willingness to use professional advertising and media techniques, most notably employing the film director Hugh Hudson to make an election broadcast that sought to counter press stereotypes by portraying the values and leadership qualities of Neil Kinnock. Cynics called the broadcast 'Kinnock. The Movie', but its impact was dramatic, adding three points to Labour's poll rating overnight. The main effect of this flying start to the

LIVERPOOL
JOHN MOORES UNIVERSITY
TRUEMAN STREET LIBRARY
TEL. 051 231 4022/4023

campaign was that Labour gained at the expense of the Alliance, whose efforts became increasingly confused. With David Owen aiming for a 'hung parliament' and David Steel talking in terms of an overall majority, the two Alliance leaders were pilloried as 'Tweedledum and Tweedledee'.[30] Labour was thus able to present itself as the main challenger, but there were few signs of serious inroads being made into Mrs Thatcher's substantial lead. At a time of low inflation, falling unemployment and rising living standards for the majority, the Prime Minister could afford to run a relatively low-key campaign, leaving her ministers to attack weak spots in Labour's armoury such as its 'Dad's Army' defence policy. In spite of 'wobbly Thursday' – occasioned by one poll showing Labour gaining ground – the Conservatives ended the campaign on the offensive, exploiting inconsistencies in statements by Kinnock and Hattersley on Labour's tax and spending plans.[31]

It therefore came as little surprise when Mrs Thatcher became the first twentieth-century leader to secure three successive election victories. On a total share of the vote that was virtually unchanged since 1983, the Conservatives gained a majority of 102 seats. Labour pushed up its share of the poll to 30.8 per cent, capturing twenty more seats, while the Alliance fell back to 22.6 per cent of the national vote. The Labour faithful were able to clutch at some straws. With a clear lead over the Alliance, Labour could at least conclude that its position as the main opposition party had been confirmed. Neil Kinnock's personal standing had been enhanced and those looking for historical parallels were able to point out that Labour had bounced back from three successive defeats in the 1950s. But there was no escape from the deep disappointment of the result. This time there were no excuses ready to hand, such as the winter of discontent or the schisms of the early 1980s. Kinnock at no stage privately believed he could win, though he did hope to cut the Tory majority more substantially, thereby giving an impression of Labour momentum. And yet in spite of an effective campaign, the party remained eleven percentage points behind the Conservatives, compared with five per cent in 1959. When Macmillan defeated Gaitskell, Labour led the Tories by nearly 30 per cent among manual workers; by 1987 that lead had narrowed to ten per cent.[32] Underpinning this picture was a debilitating failure to dent the North-South electoral divide. The Conservatives held 170 of 176 seats in the southern half of England outside London. Labour, it seems, had little to say to the home-owning, share-owning skilled workers who had lined up behind trade union reform and the sale of council houses. Proclamations of undying support for the welfare state evoked sympathy but did not translate into votes in the ballot box. Bedrock support in the old industrial areas of Scotland, Wales and northern England had been enough to stave off the Alliance challenge, but 1987 inevitably raised once again the question first posed after 1959: must Labour lose?[33]

IV

Few doubted that Labour 'must lose' for at least a year after the election. Kinnock's reaction to defeat was to press on with the type of changes he had sought to introduce since 1983. He sanctioned the party's first comprehensive policy review since the 1950s, establishing seven review groups to rethink Labour's approach both to domestic and international affairs. Inevitably, this move aroused the suspicions of those who feared a 'sell-out'. In an atmosphere of recrimination following the election, even the deputy leader joined the fray, warning that Labour should not abandon its principles simply to court short-term popularity. This, according to Hattersley, would be rather like expecting a bishop to disown the Sermon on the Mount. Kinnock met this widely held reservation head on at the annual conference in 1988:

> Let me tell this party what so many in the party tell me: the greatest concession to Thatcherism is to let it win again. Those who are afraid of developing the alternatives that will gain the support of the British people . . . had better ask themselves: if they will not pay that price for winning, what price are they prepared to pay for losing, and who are they prepared to see pay that price? Because I tell you this – the price of defeat is not paid by the people on this platform or even in this hall. The price is paid by the poor. . . . We will not have to go

creeping and crawling to the Social Fund. We will not have to wait in dead-end training. We will not have to live on low pay.[34]

Notwithstanding the Labour's leader's determination, many continued to question his capacity to succeed. A challenge to his position by Tony Benn in 1988, though easily defeated, gave the press ample opportunity to play up Labour divisions. And Kinnock himself went through a bad patch. A series of confusing statements on defence in particular added to the gloom among MPs and led to murmurings that a new leader might be needed before the next election.

Nor did the policy review, to which Benn and his allies vociferously objected, prove to be the inspirational turning point originally hoped. After lengthy deliberations, two major revisions of policy were signalled. On the domestic front, the party came to terms with the irreversibility of many Thatcherite reforms by recognising that the market economy should be regarded as innocent until found guilty, rather than vice-versa. The old certainties of nationalisation were now replaced by the idea of the government 'regulating' the economy wherever necessary. In international affairs, Labour finally modified the policy of uni-lateral nuclear disarmament that had proved so costly at the last two elections. Henceforth the party was pledged to a multilateral course of seeking to negotiate away all weapons – a reversal which Kinnock found easier to justify as a series of US-Soviet initiatives opened up the prospect of meaningful disarmament and the end of the Cold War. In many ways the review was a testament to the leader's domination of the party. Whereas Gaitskell had found that head-on confrontation made it difficult for Labour to change course, Kinnock had effectively coaxed the party machine into accepting modernisation.[35] He was easily able to dismiss left-wing accusations of betrayal, especially after humiliating Benn in the leadership contest. To the charge of having embraced Thatcher-ism, Kinnock could point out that the party was committed to redistribution of wealth, intervention in the economy and the eventual removal of nuclear weapons. More difficult to answer was the claim that the policy review had not captured the public imagination. Much of the discussion passed by ordinary voters, and press critics noted the absence of a 'big idea' to replace corporate socialism or Croslandite equality. 'It was not only metropolitan commentators who felt the absence of a theme. The most effective way of attacking Labour continued to be the insult that socialism was an out-dated creed. The review modernised the Labour Party – or started to – but failed to make socialism modern.'[36]

By the time of the completion of the policy review process in 1989, however, Labour was pulling ahead in the opinion polls. The main reason for this was the government's inept handling of the economy, notably Chancellor Nigel Lawson's encouragement of a consumer and credit-led boom that turned sour. Inflation rapidly rose towards double figures, thereby undermining the central claim of Mrs Thatcher's 'economic miracle', and the need to raise interest and mortgage rates to record levels began to punish many of the government's natural supporters. There was also a widespread feeling that, on a range of issues, the Prime Minister had gone too far. Labour seized, for example, on the proposal to introduce market mechanisms into the working of the NHS as 'privatisation run mad'; a tactic which appeared to pay off in the Vale of Glamorgan by-election of May 1989. On Europe, Mrs Thatcher's bad tempered invective about the dangers of federalism allowed Kinnock to make the running in welcoming Community initiatives, especially the social charter drafted by the French socialist Jacques Delors. Ironically, in view of the party's pledge as recently as 1983 to leave the EEC, Labour swept to a decisive victory at the European elections held in the summer of 1989 – Mrs Thatcher's first major defeat at the hands of the national electorate.[37] Most damaging of all was the Prime Minister's determination to reform local taxation by abolishing domestic rates. The introduction of the iniquitous community charge or poll tax had a catastrophic effect on the government's standing. It led to street protests in unlikely Conservative heartlands, it helped Labour to secure at Mid-Staffs its most spectacular by-election victory for fifty years, and it aroused a growing concern among Tory MPs that their three-time election winner had become a liability. Conservative fears about Labour's renewed respectability acted as an important backdrop to the events which led in November 1990 to Mrs Thatcher's resignation.[38]

Her more emollient successor John Major posed different problems for Labour. Kinnock was now confronted by 'a nice Prime Minister, a happy Cabinet, a moderate party and, above all, a successful war'.[39] Britain's participation in the United Nations conflict against Iraq was offset by the continuing effects of recession, which allowed Labour to maintain a steady but smaller lead in the polls. By the spring of 1991 political prospects had become more difficult to predict than in the dying days of the Thatcher regime. Local election results showed heavy Tory losses, though Labour had not made sufficient progress to suggest it could secure the huge swing required to deliver an outright majority. A strong showing by the Liberal Democrats, revitalised under the leadership of Paddy Ashdown, prompted much discussion of the likelihood of a hung parliament, with neither of the main parties able to dominate.[40] For several months thereafter, with the Prime Minister reluctant to call an election, Labour fortunes remained mixed. At the Monmouth by-election, the party made another gain of a sort that had been inconceivable for much of the 1980s, and confidence among activists remained high. But the nagging doubts remained. The 'Kinnock factor' was still a concern, with the Labour leader's personal popularity trailing way behind that of John Major. And some commentators questioned the wisdom of relying on the recession alone to win over voters. As one seasoned observer put it:

> Lord Wilson jettisoned both nationalisation (the cause of the parliamentary Left) and egalitarianism (the cause of the revisionist Right) and substituted science. Mr Kinnock has abandoned the accumulated rubbish of the early 1980s and replaced it with . . . well, with what?[41]

The implication was that neither a general concern for the underdog nor promises of economic competence had captured the public imagination. When John Major finally called an election in April 1992, political pundits were convinced it would be the closest contest for twenty years.

Numerous opinion polls during the three weeks of campaigning seemed to point in the same direction. By common consent, the Conservatives fought a lacklustre campaign. In comparison with his predecessor, Major's platform style was wooden and at times invited ridicule. Unable to make play with the theme of economic competence in the midst of prolonged recession, the Tories concentrated instead on undermining Labour's credibility. In particular, this meant endless repetition of the message that Labour's spending plans would mean increased personal taxation. More so than in 1987, Labour was ready for this assault and went to the lengths of issuing a 'shadow budget', proposing tax increases for higher wage earners but insisting that eight out of every ten would be better off financially. After taking the sting out of the tax issue, party strategists hoped to assert the primacy of their own chosen themes – notably the need for long-term planning and investment in industry, and for extra resources in health and education. But Labour was unable to have things all its own way. The party's use of slick media techniques backfired after its broadcast about the difficulties of receiving medical treatment turned the health service debate into petty squabbling over the 'war of Jennifer's Ear'. And with Paddy Ashdown winning plaudits for his vigorous campaigning, Neil Kinnock was forced on the defensive over Labour's attitude towards proportional representation. This meant that in the crucial final days before polling, the 'caring issues' were displaced by, on the one hand, discussion of a hung parliament, and on the other by renewed attacks from the Tory tabloids on Labour's tax plans. Nevertheless, most commentators were still predicting that Labour would at least emerge as the largest single party. They, together with the pollsters, were therefore left with egg on their face when it became clear that the Conservatives had won an unprecedented fourth victory in succession. The government's majority had fallen to 21 seats, but its share of the vote had again remained constant. Labour claimed only 35 per cent of the total poll, well short of its performance in 1979.

'So John Major turned out to be Clark Kent after all', began one of many surprised newspaper editorials.[42] The consensus of press opinion, however, was the outcome had not hinged on the mild-mannered Prime Minister's qualities, superhuman or otherwise.

Remarkably, after thirteen years of Conservative rule, it was agreed that this was an election that said more about the party of opposition. As Robert Harris wrote: 'Labour fought a good campaign, with a moderate programme and a strong team, while its opponents waged a poor campaign, had a terrible track record and a tired front bench. By all the laws of British politics, Labour should have done much better.'[43] There was some comfort to be gleaned from the party's ability to capture forty seats from the Tories, many in the 1980s barren lands of London, the south and the Midlands. But Labour still faced an electoral mountain if it was ever to climb back to power. There were only 42 seats where Labour stood in second place to the Tories by less than 4000 votes; even if all were captured, the likely effects of boundary changes would be enough to perpetuate one-party Conservative rule.[44] Nor had Labour's support among the lower social classes risen much higher than it had been in 1983. The party had not, after all, been able to recapture the hearts and minds of 'Essex man', symbolised by the voters of Basildon – a vital target seat which was held by the Tories early on election night. Commentators had no doubt that fear played a part. Aside from the fear generated by distortions about Labour's tax plans, there was also the tendency in times of economic hardship for voters to 'hold on to nurse for fear of something worse'.[45] But this fear was itself only part of a more deep-seated distrust of the Labour party. In the southern half of England at least, as the party's own post-election inquest showed, Labour had been unable to shake off its image as being incurably old fashioned and associated with the downwardly mobile. 'The harsh reality', concluded one insider, 'is that Labour is still following the road back from the disasters of 1979–83, which at heart were the real culprits of the 1992 defeat'.[46]

V

The period between the winter of discontent and the humiliation of 1983 was undoubtedly critical to the post-war decline of Labour as a governing party. What followed after the 1979 election was predictable if not predetermined. After the failings of the Wilson-Callaghan government in the 1970s, the broad church coalition of forces that had sustained Labour since the war fell apart. Unable to rely any longer on automatic trade union support, and confronted by constituency activists unrecognisable in an earlier generation, Callaghan was powerless to prevent a left-wing backlash that went far beyond that experienced by his predecessors after the defeats of 1951 and 1970. When the relative strength of the left was enhanced by the departure of disillusioned Social Democrats, the pattern of events that culminated in the 'longest suicide note in history' was set. What was almost more surprising was that Labour came back after the crushing setback of 1983. There have been attempts to argue that the formation of the SDP was vital to Labour's survival, by bringing the party to its senses and convincing it of the need to return to the political middle ground. 'In the end', claims Peter Clarke, 'Labour was to be saved not on its merits, which were shallow, but by its roots, which were deep'.[47] This line of interpretation, while recognising the residual strength of Labour support in its traditional heartlands, tends to understate the failings of the Alliance. Beset by its own internal contradictions, the Alliance lacked the necessary edge to 'break the mould'; its weakness thrown into relief by a comparison with Labour's leadership in the mid-1980s, which 'may have been a little short on ideas, but . . . was impressively long on that most crucial of political attributes, the will to win'.[48] Most determined of all to win was Neil Kinnock.

After his resignation in the wake of the 1992 election, Kinnock was described in some unlikely quarters as the most effective Labour leader since Attlee. Certainly few have moulded the party so completely in their image as did Kinnock after 1983. As the longest-serving opposition leader in British politics, he doggedly set out to modernise the party and make it once more electable. By moving against the policy and personnel of the hard left, he played a key role in reviving the Labour machine and outfacing the Alliance threat at the 1987 election. Five years on the party was unrecognisable from the routed force of 1983. The PLP, local constituency parties and trade unions were all 'Kinnockites now', lining up behind a programme that was pro-European, in favour of market economics and guardedly supportive of nuclear deterrence.[49] The electorate responded positively to this closing of the gap between public sentiment and opinion inside the Labour movement. By 1992 the Tory majority in parliament was greatly reduced; at last Labour demonstrated that it could recover ground in the Midlands, London and the south of England. But Kinnock's achievements were not enough. What was done between 1979 and 1983 could not be undone. And this inability to make Labour once more a party of power was itself in part a reflection of Kinnock's own limitations. In the first place, he was unable to eradicate the fear of Labour that underpinned the results of 1987 and 1992. His own past as a Tribunite rebel caused difficulties here; he was himself too much a product of 1970s-style Labourism to be able to escape its legacy without being accused of lacking consistency. Partly because of this, Kinnock was never quite able to make the leap between inspiring the party faithful and convincing the wider electorate. When 'addressing the nation, he somehow failed to touch the hearts and minds of the undecided'.[50] Labour had recovered, but precisely what it stood for remained elusive. 'Socialism', one front-bencher conceded in 1990, 'is what Mr Mandelson says it is'.[51]

The party's failings in the 1980s, and Neil Kinnock's inability to transcend them, might best be summarised in the distinction between Labour doctrine – its statements of official policy – and its ethos, a more nebulous combination of traditions, moods and symbols. As David Marquand has eloquently written:

> Kinnock fought his battles with the left in the realm of doctrine. He had to, for the party had no hope of winning an election until the doctrinal victories which the left had won in the early 1980s were undone. In striking contrast to Hugh Gaitskell twenty years before, he made no attempt to to challenge the party's ethos. Indeed, one of the reasons why he prevailed in the battles over doctrine was that the stubborn survival of that ethos through all the vicissitudes of the recent past played into his hands. . . . But if the resilience of the party's ethos was an asset, it was also a liability. It enabled Labour to fight off the Alliance challenge; to reassert is hold on its core constituency; to break the neo-socialist spell which had done it so much damage in the early 1980s; to embrace a new

version of the revisionism of the 1960s; and to become, once again, the only serious alternative to the Conservatives. Unfortunately, it also hampered the party's efforts to run with the grain of the technological and cultural changes which were steadily widening the gap between its core constituency and the society beyond . . . and [it] shored up the inward-looking defensiveness which cut the Labour movement off from non-Labour strands of opinion. . . . The Labour Party had faced essentially the same problem since the 1920s: . . . how to bridge the gulf between the old Labour fortresses and the potentially anti-Conservative, but non-Labour hinterland; how to construct a broad-based and enduring social coalition capable, not just of giving it a temporary majority in the House of Commons, but of sustaining a reforming government thereafter. It was nearer to solving that problem in 1990 than it had been for a quarter of a century. As seventy years of Labour history bore witness, a near-solution was not enough.[52]

CONCLUSION

Labour remained in the doldrums following the 1992 election defeat. Within a matters of months, Neil Kinnock had been replaced as party leader by the 53-year-old Scottish MP, John Smith, who had served as Shadow Chancellor under his predecessor. Smith undoubtedly had many assets. Although associated with the Labour right in his earlier career, he had not been closely embroiled in the factional disputes of the early 1980s, and had built up a reputation as a committed egalitarian, trustworthy and reassuring to the wider electorate. He was also one of very few on the opposition front bench after 1990 who could claim ministerial experience, having served as Trade Secretary in the latter stages of the Callaghan regime. As a result, Smith amassed an overwhelming 91 per cent of the electoral college vote in defeating his only rival for the leadership, Bryan Gould. The deputy leadership contest held simultaneously saw a woman, Margaret Beckett, for the first time promoted to one of the top two positions in the party hierarchy. Smith, like Kinnock before him, was clear that things would have to change if Labour fortunes were to improve. In his inaugural speech as leader, he pledged to make efforts to woo back women voters, to reform the system of trade union block votes at party conference, and to seek unity among anti-Conservative forces, though whether this meant embracing proportional representation was not specified.[1] But new faces at the top and promises of future action were not enough to restore Labour confidence; four defeats in a row had inevitably eroded the party's belief in itself. As one commentator observed, in spite of continued recession and government mismanagement of the economy, Labour MPs and 'active members are no longer altogether sure what they are doing. They know they are against the Tories, yes, but there is little else about which anyone is prepared to be very precise'.[2]

In some ways the past rather than the future seemed to offer greater comfort to the party faithful. Labour stalwarts could at least look back to the period since the end of the Second World War and point to several notable achievements with which the party was closely identified. The record of the Attlee government stands out in this respect. It was in the immediate post-war years that Labour ministers took decisive steps towards making Britain a more tolerable and humane society. The National Health Service, improved facilities in education and housing, full employment – all helped to improve the lot of working-class families after the hardships and deprivation of the war years. The importance of the welfare state in helping those whom ministers referred to as 'our people' can be gauged on the issue of poverty. Although by the time Callaghan left office there were still over a million people living below the officially measured poverty line, it was estimated that this figure would have been nearer eight million but for the comprehensive system of welfare benefits first introduced in the late 1940s.[3] In spite of the difficulties that faced subsequent Labour governments, Wilson and Callaghan could also claim to have fulfilled a reasonable proportion of their manifesto commitments. Social provision continued to expand after 1964 with the support of a progressive tax structure; conscious efforts were made to strengthen the bargaining power of workers on the shop floor; and the economic record of both the 1964 and 1970 administrations, as we have seen, was by no means as dismal as often portrayed. In the words of one television commentator, the 'stop-go' of the 1960s and 1970s was perhaps preferable to the 'stop-stop' of the late 1980s and early 1990s.[4]

But for many activists Labour's record in office has always been problematic, as Owen Hartley notes:

The party has successfully promoted and defended working-class interests as exemplified by trade unions and the public sector professional classes, had a deep concern for 'liberal' issues (as exemplified in the reforms of the 1964–70 government), had a clear and forthright view of foreign and defence policy defending British interests, and has had a potentially sound view of economic policy to which in crisis it naturally reverts: sound money, belt tightening, evenness in the distribution of misery. It is a record of which the party could be proud, but so far it cannot be.[5]

In part this was because ministers were willing to adopt policies – for example on nuclear weapons – that ran against the grain of rank-and-file sentiment. From 1951 onwards there was also a deeper undercurrent of concern: that British society was failing to evolve in a socialist direction. For those who broadly identifed 'the socialist commonwealth' with public ownership and centralised planning of the economy, the sense of disappointment was most acute. After the best endeavours of the Attlee government, over 80 per cent of Britain's industry was still privately owned, and there were few signs that nationalisation would ever extend very far beyond the service sector. Renewed optimism about economic planning in the 1960s was confounded by the rapid failure of Wilson's 'National Plan', and promises to extend state control deep into the field of manufacturing industry in the 1970s never materialised. For those within the party who were more concerned with the revisionist objective of social equality, rising living standards after the war did appear to produce a welcome levelling up within society, but no one doubted that glaring inequalities remained when Callaghan lost office. In subsequent years, of course, Attlee's legacy was undermined as the Conservatives dismantled the mixed economy through privatisation and reversed the trend of previous decades towards a modest redistribution of wealth. But prior to this a common pattern had already emerged: five or six years of Labour government left the party disgruntled and at odds with itself.

Division within the ranks has often been cited as a primary cause of Labour's electoral decline since the heady days of 1945. If the party's weakness – to return to the terms of debate used at the outset of this study – was largely the product of avoidable, contingent factors, then in fighting clearly had a part to play. Loss of office was certain to reopen ideological differences about future strategy, but this does not account for the intensity of the struggle between left and right that followed the election defeats of 1951, 1970 and 1979. Unlike the Conservative party, which responded to defeat by gradually restoring unity between competing interest groups, Labour was prepared to prolong its internecine warfare without regard for the electoral consequences. The party's failure to put its own house in order raises the question of poor leadership, which might provide another plausible means of arguing that electoral decline was an accidental process, tied to the short-comings of particular individuals. Before the middle of the 1960s, as we saw in chapter 2, the party of Attlee and Gaitskell was still a formidable fighting force. And yet in the thirteen years after 1966, under the leadership of Wilson and Callaghan, Labour lost one-sixth of its support among the working classes. The most substantial drop while the party was in office came between 1966 and 1970, when ministers 'did very nearly the opposite of what Labour voters and trade unionists expected from a Labour government'.[6] On top of pay restraint and cuts in public spending, the humiliation of devaluation, after months of 'treating sterling as the exchange equivalent of the Virgin Mary', shattered Wilson's reputation for economic competence.[7] In spite of an unhelpful inheritance, many of Labour's failings after 1974 were also self-inflicted. Callaghan's miscalculation over the timing of the 1979 election was, according to one of his own advisers, only the last of several errors, 'each of which might have been avoided', and by which 'the party progressively undermined its own capacity to govern'.[8]

But to simply point the finger of accusation at Labour's 'guilty men' in the 1960s and 1970s would, in itself, provide a far from complete explanation of the party's electoral malaise. Indeed, the case for deep seated or structural forces being paramount seems equally persuasive. There were at least three respects in which Labour's prospects were blighted by forces beyond its control. In the first place, it was no coincidence that Attlee, Wilson and Callaghan all faced acute financial crises within two years of the party coming to power, in 1947, 1966 and 1976. Economic instability, often bequeathed by an outgoing Tory government, clearly narrowed the options available to Labour ministers and highlighted Britain's vulnerability on the world stage. It was also the case, secondly, that Labour administrations were confronted by a range of hostile and powerful vested interests, such as the newspaper press and the financial markets. Perhaps most important of all, changes within post-war British society did make the task of securing a Labour majority at Westminster ever more difficult. The erosion of class barriers that came with greater affluence, though a protracted process, inevitably left its mark. Since the 1960s nearly all the predominantly Labour-supporting groups in the electorate have shrunk in size, whereas mainly Conservative supporting elements, such as the professional and managerial classes, have expanded. This alone was sufficient to reduce the Labour vote by five per cent, irrespective of any shift in voting patterns. Some political scientists have argued that the haemorrhaging of Labour support within what remained of the working class was the product of short-term dissatisfaction with policies or personnel. Others believe that the party's failure to capture more than 40 per cent of total votes cast at any election since 1970 points to a more enduring change. Whereas unionised council tenants in the old industrial heartlands might still support Labour, they were increasingly out-numbered by the mainstay of Conservative rule after 1979: the new working-class of non-unionised home-owners in southern England.[9]

The 'strange death of Labour Britain' might be best explained, in the final analysis, by a combination of both contingent, short-term errors and longer-term, structural forces. Disenchantment with the policies and divisiveness of Labour under Wilson and Callaghan proved so damaging because the party's link with those who had sustained it in an earlier generation was already under strain. Failures in office, in other words, accentuated the difficulties caused by changes in the size and composition of the electorate. What tied these together was Labour's collective inability to recognise how far the working class of the 1940s and 1950s – often materially impoverished and culturally distinct – was changing out of all recognition in the 1960s and 1970s. As James Cronin has written:

> The defeats of 1979 and, perhaps to an even greater degree, of 1983, were in this sense long in the making, and they suggest

that Labour's ensuing crisis transcends the mistakes of Callaghan and Foot, the personalities of Benn and Healey, and the good fortune of Margaret Thatcher. In essence the crisis stems from the altered relation between Labour and the working class. The ties between the class and the party, nurtured over so many years, have atrophied. Since the process has been based upon a set of very real transformations in the way working people go about their daily lives, moreover, it cannot easily be reversed. . . . In sum, the conditions that produced 1945, or 1950, or even 1964, will not recur. This is not to say that Labour is destined never to win another general election. Rather, it is to argue that Labour's future will depend crucially upon its coming to terms with the changed realities of class, and of how class is lived and experienced, in contemporary British society.[10]

Labour's overriding failure, in other words, has been its inflexibility – from the leadership downwards – in coping with 'changed realities'. Aneurin Bevan once lamented that it was the working class who had turned their back on socialism: 'History gave them their chance, and they didn't take it'. The same, we might conclude, could be said of the post-war Labour party.

NOTES

INTRODUCTION

1. A. Howard, 'We are the Masters Now', in M. Sissons and M. French (eds), *Age of Austerity 1945–1951* (London, 1963): the exact words used by Hartley Shawcross were that 'We are the masters at the moment – and . . . for a very long time to come'.
2. On structural and contingent forces, see P. Clarke, *A Question of Leadership. Gladstone to Thatcher* (London, 1991).
3. There are several general accounts of the post-war Labour party, though few as yet include coverage of the 1980s, e.g. D. Howell, *British Social Democracy. A Study in Development and Decay* (London, 1976); K. Laybourn, *The Rise of Labour. The British Labour Party 1890–1979* (London, 1988); H. Pelling, *A Short History of the Labour Party* (London, 1991 edn).
4. See, for example, the work of Lewis Minkin: *The Labour Party Conference* (London, 1978) and *The Contentious Alliance. Trade Unions and the Labour Party* (Edinburgh, 1991).
5. For an overview of the long-running debate about the relative strength of the parties in pre-1914 Britain, see G. Searle, *The Liberal Party: Triumph and Disintegration* (London, 1992).
6. R. I. McKibbin, *The Evolution of the Labour Party 1910–1924* (Oxford, 1974).
7. B. Pimlott, *Labour and the Left in the 1930s* (Cambridge, 1977).
8. A. Calder, *The People's War. Britain 1939–1945* (London, 1969).
9. P. Addison, *The Road to 1945. British Politics and the Second World War* (London, 1975); K. Jefferys, *The Churchill Coalition and Wartime Politics 1940–1945* (Manchester, 1991); S. Brooke, *Labour's War. The Labour Party and the Second World War* (Oxford, 1992).

1 LABOUR'S FINEST HOUR, 1945–51

1. See the discussion of this by P. Hennessy, 'The Attlee Governments, 1945–1951', in P. Hennessy and A. Seldon (eds), *Ruling Performance. British Governments from Attlee to Thatcher* (Oxford, 1987), pp. 31–2.

2. K. O. Morgan, *Labour in Power 1945–1951* (Oxford, 1984), p. 503. See also H. Pelling, *The Labour Governments 1945–51* (London, 1984), pp. 261–8.

3. R. Miliband, *Parliamentary Socialism* (London, 1961); J. Saville, *The Labour Movement in Britain. A Commentary* (London, 1988).

4. Cited in Hennessy and Seldon (eds), *Ruling Performance*, p. 28.

5. Douglas Jay, *Change and Fortune. A Political Record* (London, 1980), p. 135.

6. K. Jefferys (ed.), *Labour and the Wartime Coalition: From the Diary of James Chuter Ede 1941–1945* (London, 1988), p. 102: diary entry for 21 October 1942.

7. See K. O. Morgan, 'Herbert Morrison', in *Labour People. Leaders and Lieutenants: Hardie to Kinnock* (Oxford, 1987), pp. 176–88.

8. Jay, *Change and Fortune*, p. 110.

9. B. Vernon, *Ellen Wilkinson* (London, 1982), passim. For a contemporary view of Shinwell, see P. Williams (ed.), *The Diary of Hugh Gaitskell 1945–1956* (London, 1983), pp. 29–30: diary entry for 12 August 1947.

10. R. K. Alderman, 'Discipline in the Parliamentary Labour Party, 1945–51', *Parliamentary Affairs*, 18, 3 (1965), p. 304.

11. P. Seyd and P. Whiteley, *Labour's Grass Roots: The Politics of Party Membership* (Oxford, 1992), pp. 13–25.

12. Pelling, *Labour Governments*, p. 42.

13. Cited in Jay, *Change and Fortune*, p. 137.

14. B. Pimlott, *Hugh Dalton* (London, 1985), pp. 427–40.

15. A. Bullock, *The Life and Times of Ernest Bevin*, Vol. 3, *Foreign Secretary 1945–1951* (London, 1983), pp. 368–92.

16. F. S. Northedge, 'Britain and the Middle East', in R. Ovendale (ed.), *The Foreign Policy of the British Labour Governments 1945–1951* (Leicester, 1984), pp. 149–78. See also W. R. Louis, *The British Empire in the Middle East, 1945–1951* (Oxford, 1984).

17. M. Gowing, 'Britain and the Bomb. The Origins of Britain's Determination to be a Nuclear Power', *Contemporary Record*, 2, 2 (1988), pp. 36–40.

18. J. Schneer, *Labour's Conscience. The Labour Left 1945–51* (London, 1988), pp. 44–9.

19. Cited in Hugh Dalton, *High Tide and After. Memoirs 1945–60* (London, 1962), p. 64.

20. Morgan, *Labour in Power*, p. 184.

21. Jefferys, *Churchill Coalition*, pp. 170–4. See also D. N. Chester, *The Nationalisation of British Industry 1945–51* (London, 1975).

22. J. Hess, 'The Social Policy of the Attlee Government', in W. J. Mommsen (ed.), *The Emergence of the Welfare State in Britain and Germany* (London, 1981), pp. 296–311.

23. R. Barker, *Education and Politics. A Study of the Labour Party 1900–1951* (Oxford, 1972), pp. 81–97.

24. Morgan, *Labour in Power*, pp. 163–70.

25. J. Campbell, *Nye Bevan and the Mirage of British Socialism* (London, 1987), pp. 165–85.

26. A. Robertson, *The Bleak Midwinter, 1947* (Manchester, 1987), pp. 21–2.

27. For the minister's defence of his record, see Emanuel Shinwell, *I've Lived Through It All* (London, 1973), pp. 194–5.

28. Pimlott, *Hugh Dalton*, pp. 480–94.

29. K. Harris, *Attlee* (London, 1982), pp. 341–54.

30. On this theme, see H. Pelling, *Britain and the Marshall Plan* (London, 1989).

31. N. Owen, 'Attlee Governments: The End of Empire 1945–51', *Contemporary Record*, 3, 4 (1990), pp. 12–15: 'If . . . the British Empire was acquired "in a fit of absence of mind", it was lost, to judge from India's case, in a similar state of perplexity.' See also P. S. Gupta, *Imperialism and the British Labour Movement* (London, 1975) and J. Darwin, *Britain and Decolonisation* (London, 1988).

32. R. Eatwell, *The 1945–1951 Labour Governments* (London, 1979), pp. 98–9, notes the example of 'snoek', a tasteless fish purchased in bulk by the government. The public refused to eat it, and though it was claimed that the whole consignment had been sold off, rumours persisted that it had been reprocessed as cat food.

33. Morgan, 'Stafford Cripps as Chancellor', in *Labour People*, pp. 168–70.

34. See N. Rollings, 'British Budgetary Policy 1945–1954: a "Keynesian Revolution"?', *Economic History Review*, 41, 2 (1988), pp. 283–98, and references cited there.

35. Hennessy, '1949 Devaluation', *Contemporary Record*, 5, 3 (1991), pp. 483–506.

36. Morgan, *Labour in Power*, pp. 400–1.

37. H. Pelling, 'The Labour Government of 1945–1951', in M.

Bentley and J. Stevenson (eds), *High and Low Politics in Modern Britain* (Oxford, 1983), pp. 276–7.

38. H. G. Nicholas, *The British General Election of 1950* (London, 1951), pp. 296–305.

39. Dalton, *High Tide*, p. 347.

40. B. Pimlott (ed.), *The Political Diary of Hugh Dalton 1918–40, 1945–60* (London, 1986), pp. 470–1: diary entries for 25–26 February 1950.

41. Cited in Morgan, *Labour in Power*, p. 412.

42. Harris, *Attlee*, pp. 459–60.

43. Campbell, *Nye Bevan*, pp. 232–50.

44. See the conflicting views of *Tribune*, 20 April 1951 and Williams (ed.), *Gaitskell Diary*, pp. 239–57: diary entry for 30 April 1951.

45. Michael Foot, *Aneurin Bevan*, Vol. 2, *1945–60* (London, 1973), pp. 283 349; P. Williams, *Hugh Gaitskell. A Political Biography* (London, 1979), pp. 182–5.

46. Morgan, *Labour in Power*, pp. 456–61.

47. B. Donoughue and G. W. Jones, *Herbert Morrison. Portrait of a Politician* (London, 1973), pp. 471–92.

48. K. O. Morgan, *The People's Peace. British History 1945–1989* (Oxford, pp. 103–4.

49. D. Butler, *The British General Election of 1951* (London, 1952), pp. 240–8.

50. Jay, *Change and Fortune*, p. 214.

51. Pimlott, *Hugh Dalton*, pp. 605–6.

52. Saville, *Labour Movement in Britain*, p. 97.

53. D. Rubinstein, 'Socialism and the Labour Party: The Labour Left and Domestic Policy 1945–1950', in D. E. Martin and D. Rubinstein (eds), *Ideology and the Labour Movement* (London, 1979), p. 250.

54. Ian Mikardo, *Back-Bencher* (London, 1988), pp. 216–18.

55. Douglas Jay, 'The Attlee Government', *Contemporary Record*, 2, 4 (1988), p. 23.

56. A. Cairncross, *Years of Recovery. British Economic Policy 1945–51* (London, 1985), pp. 499–509.

57. P. Addison, *Now the War is Over. A Social History of Britain 1945–51* (London, 1985), p. 86.

58. N. Tiratsoo (ed.), *The Attlee Years*, (London, 1991), pp. 1–6.

59. Bullock, *Ernest Bevin*, pp. 839–48.

60. Howell, *British Social Democracy*, p. 177

2 YEARS OF OPPOSITION, 1951–64

1. J. Hinton, *Labour and Socialism. A History of the British Labour Movement 1867–1974* (Brighton, 1983), p. 179.
2. Howell, *British Social Democracy*, p. 182.
3. Miliband, *Parliamentary Socialism*, p. 331.
4. C. A. R. Crosland, *Can Labour Win?* (London, 1960), pp. 9–12. See also M. Abrams and R. Rose, *Must Labour Lose?* (Harmondsworth, 1960).
5. J. E. Cronin, *Labour and Society in Britain 1918–1979* (London, 1984), pp. 13–15.
6. J. Morgan (ed.), *The Backbench Diaries of Richard Crossman* (London, 1981), p. 31: diary entry for 6 November 1951.
7. Tom Driberg, cited in Campbell, *Nye Bevan*, p. 273. On these developments, see M. Jenkins, *Bevanism: Labour's High Tide* (Nottingham, 1979) and D. Howell, *The Rise and Fall of Bevanism* (Leeds, n.d.).
8. Mikardo, *Back-Bencher*, p. 122.
9. Harris, *Attlee*, p. 499.
10. Jay, *Change and Fortune*, p. 223.
11. Mikardo, *Back-Bencher*, p. 127.
12. Pimlott (ed.), *Dalton Diary*, p. 601: diary entry for 24–28 October 1952. On Gaitskell's Stalybridge speech, see Williams, *Hugh Gaitskell*, pp. 207–9.
13. Campbell, *Nye Bevan*, pp. 272–4.
14. B. Pimlott, 'The Labour Left', in C. Cook and I. Taylor (eds), *The Labour Party. An Introduction to its History, Structure and Politics* (London, 1980), p. 174.
15. S. Haseler, *The Gaitskellites. Revisionism in the British Labour Party* (London, 1969), pp. 6–8.
16. Jay, *Change and Fortune*, p. 221.
17. There were also those in the party, like Hugh Dalton, who believed there should be 'no guns for Huns'.
18. Pimlott (ed.), *Dalton Diary*, p. 641: diary entry for Christmas 1954.
19. Mikardo, *Back-Bencher*, p. 151.
20. E. Shaw, *Discipline and Discord in the Labour Party* (Manchester, 1988), pp. 30–50. Shaw characterises the 1950s and early 1960s as the era of 'social-democratic centralism' in party management, when the 'tanks' at Transport House ensured strict discipline. He notes (p. 295) that in the 1980s 'disciplinarians from this period, like Denis Healey (who had favoured Bevan's expulsion) embraced "tolerance" . . . and "the right of dissent"

when they found themselves in the minority, were treated with cold scepticism by left-wing veterans of the Bevanite wars'.

21. Cited in Pimlott, *Hugh Dalton*, p. 619.
22. Pimlott (ed.), *Dalton Diary*, p. 671: diary entry for 26 May 1955.
23. D. Butler, *The British General Election of 1955* (London, 1955), pp. 82–94 and 160; Pelling, *Short History of the Labour Party*, p. 114.
24. L. Hunter, *The Road to Brighton Pier* (London, 1959), p. 222.
25. Pimlott, *Hugh Dalton*, pp. 622–3.
26. The full result was Gaitskell 157 votes, Bevan 70, Morrison 40.
27. Jay, *Change and Fortune*, p. 247.
28. Denis Healey, *The Time of My Life* (London, 1989), p. 154.
29. Williams, *Hugh Gaitskell*, pp. 278–92.
30. C. A. R. Crosland, *The Future of Socialism* (London, 1956), p. 102ff. For an assessment, see G. Foote, *The Labour Party's Political Thought* (London, 1985), pp. 212–20.
31. Cited in Campbell, *Nye Bevan*, p. 312.
32. On this theme, see D. Widgery, *The Left in Britain 1956–68* (Harmondsworth, 1976).
33. Campbell, Nye Bevan, p. 331.
34. Foot, *Aneurin Bevan*, pp. 569–71.
35. Haseler, *The Gaitskellites*, pp. 99–111.
36. C. Cook and J. Ramsden (eds), *By-Elections in British Politics* (London, 1975), pp. 195–6.
37. Campbell, *Nye Bevan*, p. 358.
38. D. Butler and R. Rose, *The British General Election of 1959* (London, 1960), pp. 189–201.
39. Howell, *British Social Democracy*, p. 219.
40. Jay, *Change and Fortune*, pp. 272–5.
41. H. M. Drucker, *Doctrine and Ethos in the Labour Party* (London, 1979) pp. 8–10.
42. I. McLean, 'Labour since 1945', in C. Cook and J. Ramsden (eds), *Trends in British Politics since 1945* (London, 1978), p. 48.
43. S. Crosland, *Tony Crosland* (London, 1982), p. 93.
44. D. Marquand, *The Progressive Dilemma. From Lloyd George to Kinnock* (London, 1991), pp. 133–4.
45. Gaitskell secured 161 votes to Wilson's 88. The price of Wilson's challenge, however, was that it made him several enemies within the party who were later to haunt his own leadership.
46. Cited in Crosland, *Tony Crosland*, p. 104.
47. B. Brivati, 'Campaign for Democratic Socialism', *Contemporary Record*, 4, 1 (1990), pp. 11–12.
48. P. Anderson, 'The Left in the Fifties', *New Left Review*, 29 (1965), pp. 8–9: 'Instead of calling for a structural extension of

the public sector by a wide transfer of existing industries from private to public ownership, it in effect proposed to build up the public sector alongside an intact private sector, by creating new public enterprises in the "science-based" and "growth" industries, where the government already finances the bulk of research. The idea was, politically, a small masterpiece.'

49. L. J. Robins, *The Reluctant Party. Labour and the EEC 1961–75* (Ormskirk, 1979), pp. 11–38.

50. Morgan, *Labour People*, pp. 249–51.

51. Morgan, *People's Peace*, p. 231.

52. A. Howard and R. West, *The Making of a Prime Minister* (London, 1965), p. 38.

53. D. Butler and A. King, *The British General Election of 1964* (London, 1965), pp. 110–16; A. Howard, *Crossman. The Pursuit of Power* (London, 1990), pp. 262–4.

54. See J. Goldthorpe *et al.*, *The Affluent Worker. Political Attitudes and Behaviour* (Cambridge, 1968).

55. N. Tiratsoo, *Reconstruction, Affluence and Labour Politics. Coventry 1945–60* (London, 1990), pp. 110–20.

56. Cronin, *Labour and Society in Britain*, pp. 172–4.

57. Charles Curran MP, cited in Campbell, *Nye Bevan*, p. 372.

58. T. Jones, 'Labour Revisionism and Public Ownership 1951–63', *Contemporary Record*, 5, 3 (1991), pp. 443–6.

59. Jay, *Change and Fortune*, pp. 287–8; Williams, *Hugh Gaitskell*, pp. 447–55.

60. T. Nairn, 'Hugh Gaitskell', *New Left Review*, 25 (1964), p. 63.

61. Clarke, *Question of Leadership*, p. 255.

3   THE WILSON GOVERNMENTS, 1964–70

1. Cited in Joe Haines, *The Politics of Power* (London, 1977), p. 222.

2. K. O. Morgan, 'The Wilson Years 1964–70', *Contemporary Record*, 3, 4 (1990), p. 22. For a hostile view, see also A. Morgan, *Harold Wilson* (London, 1992).

3. Howell, *British Social Democracy*, p. 245.

4. D. Walker, 'The First Wilson Governments, 1964–70', in Hennessy and Seldon (eds), *Ruling Performance*, pp. 186–209. A more sympathetic account is also found in B. Pimlott, *Harold Wilson* (London, 1992), which appeared too late for full consideration in this chapter.

5. Marquand, *Progressive Dilemma*, p. 158.

6. Marcia Williams, *Inside Number Ten* (London, 1972), p. 203.

7.   J. Margach, *The Abuse of Power* (London, 1978), p. 177.

8.   Haines, *Politics of Power*, pp. 158–87.

9.   S. Brittan, *Steering the Economy: the Role of the Treasury* (Harmondsworth, 1971), p. 293.

10.   James Callaghan, *Time and Chance* (London, 1987), p. 160.

11.   George Brown, *In My Way* (London, 1971), pp. 90–9.

12.   Jay, *Change and Fortune*, pp. 324–5.

13.   Cited in P. Whitehead, *The Writing on the Wall: Britain in the Seventies* (London, 1985), p. 4.

14.   C. Ponting, *Breach of Promise. Labour in Power 1964–1970* (London, 1989), pp. 44–54.

15.   D. Childs, *Britain since 1945. A Political History* (London, 1986 edn), pp. 167–9.

16.   Crosland, *Tony Crosland*, p. 148, cites the education minister's notorious comment: 'If it's the last thing I do, I'm going to destroy every fucking grammar school in England'.

17.   Cook and Ramsden (eds), *By-Elections in British Politics*, pp. 228–9.

18.   D. Butler and A. King, *The British General Election of 1966* (London, pp. 178–82.

19.   Ibid., pp. 259–67.

20.   Lord Wigg, *George Wigg* (London, 1972), p. 329.

21.   Tony Benn, *Out of the Wilderness: Diaries, 1963–67* (London, 1987), p. 397: diary entry for 13 March 1966.

22.   G. Goodman, *The Awkward Warrior. Frank Cousins: His Life and Times* (London, 1979), pp. 478–501.

23.   Jay, *Change and Fortune*, pp. 344–45.

24.   Barbara Castle, *The Castle Diaries 1964–1976* (London, 1990 edn), p. 75: diary entry for 18 July 1966.

25.   W. Beckerman (ed.), *The Labour Government's Economic Record 1964–1970* (London, 1972), pp. 59–64.

26.   Cited in Whitehead, *Writing on the Wall*, p. 7. See also Brown, *In My Way*, pp. 113–17.

27.   Marquand, *Progressive Dilemma*, p. 161.

28.   A. Howard (ed.), *The Crossman Diaries. Selections from the Diaries of a Cabinet Minister 1964–1970* (London, 1979), p. 209: diary entry for 24 July 1966.

29.   Williams, *Inside Number Ten*, pp. 209–10.

30.   Jay, *Change and Fortune*, p. 406.

31.   Cited in Howell, *British Social Democracy*, p. 270.

32.   Roy Jenkins, *A Life at the Centre* (London, 1991), pp. 208–10.

33.   Cited in D. McKie and C. Cook (eds), *Decade of Disillusion. British Politics in the Sixties* (London, 1972), p. 192.

34. Cook and Ramsden (eds), *By-Elections in British Politics*, p. 223.
35. Howard (ed.), *Crossman Diaries*, pp. 253–4: diary entry for 11 December 1966.
36. Jenkins, *Life at the Centre*, p. 258.
37. Cited in Whitehead, *Writing on the Wall*, pp. 20–1.
38. For a full discussion of *In Place of Strife*, see P. Jenkins, *The Battle of Downing Street* (London, 1970), pp. 26–43.
39. Mikardo, *Back-Bencher*, p. 176.
40. Jenkins, *Battle of Downing Street*, p. 140, cites Wilson's response to the claim of union leader Hugh Scanlon that no one wanted the Prime Minister to become another Ramsay MacDonald: 'I have no intention of becoming another Ramsay MacDonald. Nor do I intend to be another Dubcek. Get your tanks off my lawn Hughie!'
41. Tony Benn, *Office Without Power: Diaries, 1968–72* (London, 1988), p. 166: diary entry for 8 May 1969.
42. A. Sked and C. Cook, *Post-War Britain. A Political History* (Harmondsworth, 1979), p. 162: 'Solomon Binding' subsequently became a nickname for agreements that amounted to little more than a face saving formula.
43. D. Barnes and E. Reid, *Government and Trade Unions: the British Experience 1964–79* (London, 1980), p. 128.
44. Laybourn, *Rise of Labour*, p. 163.
45. Ponting, *Breach of Promise*, p. 384.
46. Whitehead, *Writing on the Wall*, p. 44.
47. Jenkins, *Life at the Centre*, p. 300.
48. D. Butler and M. Pinto-Duschinsky, *The British General Election of 1970* (London, 1971), pp. 337–51.
49. Jay, *Change and Fortune*, p. 410.
50. B. Lapping, *The Labour Government 1966–1970* (Harmondsworth, 1970), p. 186.
51. Beckerman (ed.), *Labour Government's Economic Record*, pp. 40–2.
52. Mikardo, *Back-Bencher*, pp. 181–2, found from knocking on doors after the election that of a randon sample of 116 people who supported Labour in 1966, 111 did not vote in 1970.
53. Anthony Crosland, *Socialism Now*, (London, 1974) pp. 15–58. The failure of the DEA was, however, offset to an extent by the unsung successes of the Ministry of Technology – see R. Coopey, 'The White Heat of Scientific Revolution', *Contemporary Record*, 5, 1 (1991), pp. 115–27.
54. This theme runs through Harold Wilson, *The Labour Government 1964–1970. A Personal Record* (London, 1971).
55. Crosland, *Tony Crosland*, p. 184. Another of Wilson's enemies

once commented: 'There are two things I dislike about Harold: his face' cited in P. Kellner and C. Hitchens, *Callaghan: The Road to No. 10* (London, 1976), p. 180.

56.   Healey, *Time of My Life*, pp. 331 and 336.

57.   B. Hindess, *The Decline of Working-Class Politics* (London, 1971), provided evidence based upon a study of local Labour branches in Liverpool. See also the same author's 'The Decline of Working-Class Politics: A Reappraisal', in B. Pimlott and C. Cook (eds), *Trade Unions in British Politics* (London, 1991).

58.   Jenkins, *Battle of Downing Street*, p. 160.

59.   M. Franklin, *The Decline of Class Voting in Britain* (Oxford, 1985), p. 153. See also D. Butler and D. Stokes, *Political Change in Britain* (London, 1974 edn), pp. 409–19.

60.   Morgan, *Labour People*, p. 261.

61.   Marquand, *Progressive Dilemma*, p. 158.

4 'CRISIS. WHAT CRISIS?', 1970–79

1.   K. Coates (ed.), *What Went Wrong* (Nottingham, 1979), p. 7.

2.   See, for example, J. Barnett, *Inside the Treasury* (London, 1982) and B. Donoughue, *Prime Minister. The Conduct of Policy under Harold Wilson and James Callaghan, 1974–79* (London, 1987).

3.   Marquand, *Progressive Dilemma*, pp. 158 and 174.

4.   M. Holmes, *The Labour Government, 1974–79* (London, 1985), p. 1.

5.   D. Coates, *Labour in Power?* (London, 1980), pp. 154–61.

6.   Healey, *Time of My Life*, pp. 372–64; M. Artis and D. Cobham (eds), *Labour's Economic Policies 1974–1979* (Manchester, 1991), pp. 266–77.

7.   A. J. Taylor, *The Trade Unions and the Labour Party* (London, 1987), pp. 6–10.

8.   Jenkins, *Life at the Centre*, pp. 327–49.

9.   Crosland, *Tony Crosland*, p. 229: he was not opposed to the European Community, but thought it was less important than many other things to his Grimsby constituents.

10.   P. Whitehead, 'The Labour Governments, 1974–79', in Hennessy and Seldon (eds), *Ruling Performance*, p. 243.

11.   Cronin, *Labour and Society in Britain*, pp. 202–4.

12.   Morgan, *People's Peace*, p. 346.

13.   Margach, *Abuse of Power*, p. 155.

14.   M. Hatfield, *The House the Left Built. Inside Labour Policy-Making 1970–75* (London, 1978), p. 228. On the Lincoln by-election, see P. Seyd, 'The Tavernite', *Political Quarterly*, 45 (1974), pp. 243–6.

15. Haines, *Politics of Power*, pp. 189–90.

16. D. Butler and D. Kavanagh, *The British General Election of February 1974* (London, 1974), pp. 272–3: the combined share of the vote held by the two main parties, which had never been less than 89 per cent since the war, now fell to 76 per cent.

17. This theme is spelt out by Crosland in *Socialism Now*, pp. 22ff.

18. Barnett, *Inside the Treasury*, p. 23.

19. M. Artis, D. Cobham and M. Wickham-Jones, 'Social Democracy in Hard Times. The Economic Record of the Labour Government 1974–1979', *Twentieth Century British History*, 3, 1 (1992), pp. 39–43.

20. Whitehead, *Writing on the Wall*, p. 132.

21. D. Butler and D. Kavanagh, *The British General Election of October 1974* (London, 1985), pp. 272–81.

22. Jay, *Change and Fortune*, p. 484.

23. Robins, *Reluctant Party*, pp. 127–9.

24. Barnett, *Inside the Treasury*, p. 49.

25. Crosland, *Tony Crosland*, pp. 288–97.

26. Donoughue, *The Conduct of Policy*, p.3.

27. D. Leigh, *The Wilson Plot. The Intelligence Services and the Discrediting of a Prime Minister* (London, 1988), pp. 2–5. See also S. Dorril and R. Ramsay, *Smear. Wilson and the Secret State* (London, 1991).

28. Harold Wilson, *Final Term. The Labour Government, 1974–1976* (London, 1979), p. 17.

29. Whitehead, in Hennessy and Seldon (eds), *Ruling Performance*, p. 254. On the liberalisation of 'centralist' methods of party control, see Shaw, *Discipline and Discord*, pp. 295–6.

30. Howell, *British Social Democracy*, p. 297.

31. Denis Healey, cited in Hennessy and Seldon (eds), *Ruling Performance*, p. 255.

32. Kellner and Hitchens, *Callaghan*, p. 175–8.

33. Crosland, *Tony Crosland*, pp. 355–6.

34. Whitehead, *Writing on the Wall*, p. 187, citing Gavyn Davies of the Downing Street Policy Unit.

35. For full descriptions of cabinet debates on the crisis, see K. Burk and A. Cairncross, *'Goodbye Great Britain'. The 1976 IMF Crisis* (London and New Haven, 1992), pp. 20–110, and Edmund Dell, *A Hard Pounding. Politics and Economic Crisis 1974–1976* (Oxford, 1991), pp. 264–75.

36. Cited in S. Fay and H. Young, *The Day the £ Nearly Died* (London, 1978), pp. 40–1.

37. Elements within the US government were determined that

Britain should put its economic house in order; talk of conspiracy can be found in the recollections of leading participants, recorded in the symposium '1976 IMF Crisis', *Contemporary Record*, 3, 2 (1989), p. 43.

38. A. Michie and S. Hoggart, *The Pact: the Inside Story of the Lib-Lab Government, 1977–8* (London, 1978), p. 183.

39. Healey, *Time of My Life*, p. 433.

40. Cited in R. Harris, *The Making of Neil Kinnock* (London, 1984), p. 96.

41. Morgan, *People's Peace*, p. 390; P. Whiteley, 'The Decline of Labour's Local Party Membership and Electoral Base, 1945–79', in D. Kavanagh (ed.), *The Politics of the Labour Party* (London, 1982), pp. 111–32.

42. P. Whiteley, *The Labour Party in Crisis* (London, 1983), p. 130.

43. A. Young, *The Reselection of MPs* (London, 1983), pp. 103–10.

44. Cited in David Steel, *A House Divided* (London, 1980), p. 125.

45. The comment of a former Permanent Secretary at the Department of Employment, cited in Barnes and Reid, *Government and Trade Unions*, p. 212.

46. Callaghan, *Time and Chance*, pp. 514–16.

47. Harris, *Making of Neil Kinnock*, pp. 116–17.

48. Callaghan's actual words, after returning from a foreign summit, were: 'I don't think that other people in the world would share the view that that there is mounting chaos.'

49. Taylor, *Trade Unions and the Labour Party*, pp. 106–7.

50. B. Butler and D. Kavanagh, *The British General Election of 1979* (London, 1980) pp. 336–9.

51. Whitehead, in Hennessy and Seldon (eds), *Ruling Performance*, p. 264.

52. Artis, Cobham and Wickham-Jones, 'Social Democracy in Hard Times', *Twentieth Century British History*, p. 58.

53. I. Crewe, 'The Labour Party and the Electorate', in Kavanagh (ed.), *Politics of the Labour Party*, pp. 10–11.

54. Butler and Kavanagh, *General Election of 1979*, pp. 340–8.

55. On this theme, see I. Crewe and B. Sarlvik, *Decade of Dealignment: the Conservative Victory of 1979 and Electoral Trends in the 1970s* (Cambridge, 1983).

56. Healey, *Time of My Life*, p. 462.

57. Coates (ed.), *What Went Wrong*, p. 29.

58. On Scottish devolution, see F. Wood, 'Scottish Labour in Government and Opposition: 1964–79', in I. Donnachie, C. Harvie and I. Woods (eds), *Forward. Labour Politics in Scotland 1888–1988* (Edinburgh, 1989), pp. 122–9.

59. Neil Kinnock, cited in Harris, *Making of Neil Kinnock*, p. 114.

60. Drucker, *Doctrine and Ethos in the Labour Party*, p. 110.

61. David Marquand, 'Inquest on a Movement', *Encounter*, July 1979.

5 THE END OF THE ROAD?, 1979–92

1. Marquand, *Progressive Dilemma*, p. 193.

2. Peter Shore, cited in Whitehead, *Writing on the Wall*, p. 350.

3. D. Kogan and M. Kogan, *The Battle for the Labour Party* (London, 1982), pp. 68–9.

4. Tom Litterick, formerly MP for Selly Oak, cited in Whitehead, *Writing on the Wall*, p. 349.

5. Austin Mitchell, *Four Years in the Death of the Labour Party* (London, 1983), p. 26.

6. G. L. Williams and A. L. Williams, *Labour's Decline and the Social Democrats' Fall* (London, 1989), pp. 2–6.

7. Whitehead, *Writing on the Wall*, p. 355.

8. Mitchell, *Four Years in the Death of the Labour Party*, p. 117.

9. S. Hoggart and D. Leigh, *Michael Foot. A Portrait* (London, 1981), p. 2. See also H. Drucker, 'Changes in the Labour Party Leadership', *Parliamentary Affairs*, 34 (1981), pp. 369–91.

10. Healey, *Time of My Life*, p. 477.

11. Jon Lansman, cited in Kogan and Kogan, *Battle for the Labour Party*, p. 97.

12. Giles Radice MP, cited in Healey, *Time of My Life*, p. 484. See also J. Adams, *Tony Benn*, (London, 1992), pp. 407–17.

13. Harris, *Making of Neil Kinnock*, pp. 149–50.

14. M. Crick, *Militant* (London, 1984), pp. 171–84. Shaw, *Discipline and Discord*, pp. 298–9, notes that the reassertion of managerial control was rendered difficult by various factors, such as the composition of local party membership, legal hurdles and the reluctance of many MPs to return to discredited disciplinary techniques.

15. J. Gyford, *The Politics of Local Socialism* (London, 1985), pp. 14–20.

16. D. Butler and D. Kavanagh, *The British General Election of 1983* (London, 1984), p. 58.

17. Harris, *Making of Neil Kinnock*, p. 203. Michael Foot's defence of his handling of the campaign is set out in *Another Heart and Other Pulses* (London, 1984).

18. Mitchell, *Four Years in the Death of the Labour Party*, p. 2.

19. Butler and Kavanagh, *General Election of 1983*, p. 293.

20. G. M. F. Drover, *Neil Kinnock. The Path to the Leadership* (London, 1984), p. 134.

21. Hattersley captured 67 per cent of the vote for the deputy leadership, compared with 27 per cent for his nearest rival, Michael Meacher.

22. Drover, *Neil Kinnock*, p. 137.

23. Shaw, *Discipline and Discord*, pp. 299–302.

24. K. Laybourn, *A History of British Trade Unionism c.1770–1990* Gloucester, 1992), p. 208: union membership was to fall from over thirteen million to ten million in the decade after 1979. In the first half of the 1980s, the proportion of the workforce which was unionised fell from 57.3 per cent to 49.5 per cent.

25. P. Seyd, *The Rise and Fall of the Labour Left* (London, 1987), pp. 169 70.

26. Drover, *Neil Kinnock*, p. 144.

27. Morgan, *Labour People*, p. 338.

28. G. Goodman, *The Miners' Strike* (London, 1985), pp. 110–16. See also M. Adeney and J. Lloyd, *The Miners' Strike, 1984–5. Loss without Limit* (London, 1987).

29. C. Hughes and P. Wintour, *Labour Rebuilt. The New Model Party* (London, 1990), pp. 14–16.

30. J. D. Derbyshire and I. Derbyshire, *Politics in Britain from Callaghan to Thatcher* (London, 1988), pp. 152–61.

31. R. Tyler, *Campaign* (London, 1987), pp. 135–40.

32. I. Crewe, 'Has the Two-Party System Returned?', *Contemporary Record*, 4, 4 (1991), p. 15.

33. D. Butler and D. Kavanagh, *The British General Election of 1987* (London, 1988), pp. 265–71.

34. Hughes and Wintour, *Labour Rebuilt*, pp. 202–3.

35. P. Kellner, 'Labour Adaptions since 1979', *Contemporary Record*, 3, 2 (1990), pp. 13–15.

36. Hughes and Wintour, *Labour Rebuilt*, p. 205.

37. Morgan, *People's Peace*, pp. 502–3.

38. M. Wickham-Jones and D. Shell, 'What Went Wrong? The Fall of Mrs Thatcher', *Contemporary Record*, 5, 2 (1991), pp. 321–39.

39. *Observer*, 17 March 1991.

40. *The Guardian*, 4 May 1991.

41. Alan Watkins, in the *Observer*, 12 January 1992.

42. *Sunday Times*, 12 April 1992.

43. Ibid.

44. *New Statesman and Society*, 17 April 1992.

45. Hugo Young, in *The Guardian*, 11 April 1992.

46. Tom Sawyer, chairman of the NEC Home Policy Committee, cited in *The Guardian*, 18 June 1992.
47. Clarke, *Question of Leadership*, p. 275.
48. Marquand, *Progressive Dilemma*, p. 193.
49. Seyd and Whiteley, *Labour's Grass Roots*, pp. 118–45, demonstrate that from the mid-1980s onwards the views of local party members on major policy issues gradually came back into line with those of the national leadership.
50. Hugo Young, *The Guardian*, 18 July 1992.
51. Ibid., 13 June 1990: this was a variation on the comment of Mandelson's grandfather, Herbert Morrison, who once defined socialism as 'what a Labour government does'.
52. Marquand, *Progressive Dilemma*, pp. 197 and 206–7.

CONCLUSION

1. *Observer*, 19 July 1992.
2. Julia Langdon, in *The Guardian*, 11 August 1992.
3. D. Steel, 'Labour in Office: the Post-War Experience', in Cook and Taylor (eds), *The Labour Party*, pp. 154–9.
4. A comment made by the BBC's Economic Editor, Peter Jay, during the sterling crisis of September 1992.
5. O. Hartley, 'Labour Governments 1924–79', *Contemporary Record*, 3, 4 (1990), p. 25.
6. E. Hobsbawm, 'Observations on the Debate', in M. Jacques and F. Mulhearn (eds), *The Forward March of Labour Halted?* (London, 1981).
7. Edward Pearce, *The Gaurdian*, 6 May 1992.
8. Donoughue, *Conduct of Policy*, p. 189. Alan Watkins once reflected that 'of all the political decisions Lord Callaghan took, every single one turned out to be wrong' – *Observer*, 16 April 1989.
9. I. Crewe, 'Voting Patterns since 1959', *Contemporary Record*, 2, 4, (1988). For the idea of 'trendless fluctuations' in voting patterns, see A. Heath, R. Jowell and J. Curtice, *How Britain Votes* (Oxford, 1985), and A. Heath *et al.*, *Understanding Political Change* (Oxford), 1990), esp. pp. 1–9.
10. Cronin, *Labour and Society in Britain*, p. 208.

SELECT BIBLIOGRAPHY

This highly selective list of books is intended as a guide to further reading; some of the many important journal articles on post-war Labour politics are cited in the Notes.

GENERAL SECONDARY WORKS

J. Callaghan, *Socialism in Britain since 1884* (Oxford, 1990).

C. Cook and I. Taylor (eds), *The Labour Party. An Introduction to its History, Structure and Politics* (London, 1980).

J. E. Cronin, *Labour and Society in Britain 1918–1979* (London, 1984).

A. J. Davies, *To Build a New Jerusalem. The British Labour Movement from the 1880s to the 1990s* (London, 1992).

P. Hennessy and A. Seldon (eds), *Ruling Performance. British Governments from Attlee to Thatcher* (Oxford, 1987).

J. Hinton, *Labour and Socialism. A History of the British Labour Movement 1867–1974* (Brighton, 1983).

D. Howell, *British Social Democracy. A Study in Development and Decay* (London, 1976).

D. Kavanagh (ed.), *The Politics of the Labour Party* (London, 1982).

K. Laybourn, *The Rise of Labour. The British Labour Party 1890–1979* (London, 1988).

R. Miliband, *Parliamentary Socialism. A Study in the Politics of Labour* (London, 1961).

K. O. Morgan, *The People's Peace. British History 1945–1989* (Oxford, 1990).

H. Pelling, *A Short History of the Labour Party* (London, 1991 edn).

J. Saville, *The Labour Movement in Britain. A Commentary* (London, 1988).

1945–1951

A. Cairncross, *Years of Recovery: British Economic Policy 1945–51* (London, 1985).

R. Eatwell, *The 1945–1951 Labour Governments* (London, 1979).

P. Hennessy, *Never Again. Britain 1945–1951* (London, 1992).

K. Jefferys, *The Attlee Governments 1945–1951* (London, 1992).

K. O. Morgan, *Labour in Power 1945–1951* (Oxford, 1984).

H. Pelling, *The Labour Governments 1945–51* (London, 1984).

A. Robertson, *The Bleak Midwinter, 1947* (Manchester, 1987).

A. A. Rogow and P. Shore, *The Labour Government and British Industry, 1945–51* (London, 1955).

J. Schneer, *Labour's Conscience. The Labour Left 1945–51* (London, 1988).

M. Sissons and P. French (eds), *Age of Austerity 1945–51* (London, 1963).

N. Tiratsoo (ed.), *The Attlee Years* (London, 1991).

1951–1964

S. Haseler, *The Gaitskellites. Revisionism in the British Labour Party, 1951–64* (London, 1969).

D. Howell, *The Rise and Fall of Bevanism* (Leeds, n.d).

L. Hunter, *The Road to Brighton Pier* (London, 1959).

M. Jenkins, *Bevanism: Labour's High Tide* (Nottingham, 1979).

D. Widgery, *The Left in Britain 1956–68* (Harmondsworth, 1976).

1964–1970

W. Beckerman (ed.), *The Labour Government's Economic Record 1964–1970* (London, 1972).

S. Brittan, *Steering the Economy: the Role of the Treasury* (Harmondsworth, 1971).

S. Dorril and R. Ramsey, *Smear. Wilson and the Secret State* (London, 1991).

P. Jenkins, *The Battle of Downing Street* (London, 1970).

B. Lapping, *The Labour Government 1966–1970* (Harmondsworth, 1970).

D. Leigh, *The Wilson Plot. The Intelligence Services and the Discrediting of a Prime Minister* (London, 1988).

C. Ponting, *Breach of Promise. Labour in Power 1964–1970* (London, 1989).

M. Stewart, *The Jekyll and Hyde Years. Politics and Economic Policy since 1964* (London, 1977).

1970–1979

M. Artis and D. Cobham (eds), *Labour's Economic Policies 1974–1979* (Manchester, 1991).

N. Bosanquet and P. Townsend (eds), *Labour and Equality: a Fabian Study of Labour in Power, 1974–79* (London, 1980).

K. Burk and A. Cairncross, *'Goodbye, Great Britain'. The 1976 IMF Crisis* (London and New Haven, 1992).

B. Donoughue, *Prime Minister. The Conduct of Policy under Harold Wilson and James Callaghan, 1974–79* (London, 1987).

D. Coates, *Labour in Power? A Study of the Labour Government 1974–1979* (London, 1980).

K. Coates (ed.), *What Went Wrong. Explaining the Fall of the Labour Government* (Nottingham, 1979).

M. Holmes, *The Labour Government, 1974–79. Political Aims and Economic Reality* (London, 1985).

M. Hatfield, *The House the Left Built. Inside Labour Policy-Making 1970–1975* (London, 1978).

A. Michie and S. Hoggart, *The Pact: the Inside Story of the Lib-Lab Government, 1977–8* (London, 1978).

P. Whitehead, *The Writing on the Wall: Britain in the Seventies* (London, 1985).

1979–1992

M. Crick, *Militant* (London, 1984).

G. Hodgson, *Labour at the Crossroads. The Political and Economic Challenge to the Labour Party in the 1980s* (Oxford, 1981).

C. Hughes and P. Wintour, *Labour Rebuilt. The New Model Party* (London, 1990).

M. Jacques and F. Mulhearn (eds), *The Forward March of Labour Halted?* (London, 1981).

P. Jenkins, *Mrs Thatcher's Revolution. The Ending of the Socialist Era* (London, 1987).

D. Kogan and M. Kogan, *The Battle for the Labour Party* (London, 1982).
P. Seyd, *The Rise and Fall of the Labour Left* (London, 1987).
P. Whiteley, *The Labour Party in Crisis* (London, 1983).

POLICY AND IDEOLOGY

R. Barker, *Education and Politics: a Study of the Labour Party 1900–1951* (Oxford, 1972).
H. M. Drucker, *Doctrine and Ethos in the Labour Party* (London, 1979).
G. Foote, *The Labour Party's Political Thought* (London, 1985).
P. S. Gupta, *Imperialism and the British Labour Movement, 1914–1964* (London, 1975).
D. E. Martin and D. Rubinstein (eds), *Ideology and the Labour Movement: Essays Presented to John Saville* (London, 1979).
R. Ovendale (ed.), *The Foreign Policy of the British Labour Governments 1945–1951* (Leicester, 1984).
L. J. Robins, *The Reluctant Party. Labour and the EEC 1961–75* (Ormskirk, 1979).
A. Warde, *Consensus and Beyond: the Development of Labour Party Strategy since the Second World War* (Manchester, 1982).

(See also under chronological sections above for works on economic policy)

PARTY ORGANISATION

R. T. Mckenzie, *British Political Parties. The Distribution of Power within the Conservative and Labour Parties* (London, 1955).
L. Minkin, *The Labour Party Conference. A Study in the Politics of Intra-Party Democracy* (London, 1978).
M. Rush, *The Selection of Parliamentary Candidates* (London, 1969).
E. Shaw, *Discipline and Discord in the Labour Party. The Politics of Managerial Control in the Labour Party, 1951–87* (Manchester, 1988).
A. Young, *The Reselection of MPs* (London, 1983).

TRADE UNIONISM

D. Barnes and E. Reid, *Government and Trade Unions: the British Experience 1964–79* (London, 1980).

M. Harrison, *Trade Unionism and the Labour Party since 1945* (London, 1960).

K. Laybourn, *A History of British Trade Unionism c.1770–1990* (Gloucester, 1992).

L. Minkin, *The Contentious Alliance. Trade Unions and the Labour Party* (Edinburgh, 1991).

L. Panitch, *Social Democracy and Industrial Militancy: the Labour Party, the Trade Unions and Incomes Policy, 1945–74* (Cambridge, 1976).

B. Pimlott and C. Cook (eds), *Trade Unions in British Politics. The First 250 Years* (London, 1991)

R. Price, *Labour in British Society. An Interpretative History* (London, 1986).

A. J. Taylor, *The Trade Unions and the Labour Party* (London, 1987).

LOCAL POLITICS

I. Donnachie, C. Harvie and I. Woods (eds), *Forward. Labour Politics in Scotland 1888–1988* (Edinburgh, 1989).

J. Grayson, *Solid Labour: a Short History of the Yorkshire Regional Council of the Labour Party, 1941–91* (Wakefield, 1991).

J. Gyford, *The Politics of Local Socialism* (London, 1985).

B. Hindess, *The Decline of Working-Class Politics* (London, 1971).

E. Janosik, *Constituency Labour Parties in British Politics* (London, 1968).

P. Seyd and P. Whiteley, *Labour's Grass Roots: The Politics of Party Membership* (Oxford, 1992).

N. Tiratsoo, *Reconstruction, Affluence and Labour Politics. Coventry 1945–60* (London, 1990).

J. E. Turner, *Labour's Doorstep Politics in London* (London, 1978).

ELECTIONS AND VOTING PATTERNS

M. Abrams and R. Rose, *Must Labour Lose?* (Harmondsworth, 1960)

D. Butler and D. Stokes, *Political Change in Britain* (London, 1974 edn).

C. Cook and J. Ramsden (eds), *By-Elections in British Politics* (London, 1973).

I. Crewe and B. Sarlvik, *Decade of Dealignment: the Conservative Victory of 1979 and Electoral Trends in the 1970s* (Cambridge, 1983).

M. Franklin, *The Decline of Class Voting in Britain. Changes in the Basis of Electoral Choice, 1964–1983* (Oxford, 1985).

A. Heath, R. Jowell and J. Curtice, *How Britain Votes* (Oxford, 1985).

A. Heath et. al., *Understanding Political Change. Voting Behaviour in* Britain 1964–87 (Oxford, 1990).

D. Robertson, *Class and the British Electorate* (Oxford, 1984).

R. Rose and I. McAllister, *Voters Begin to Choose: From Closed Class to Open Elections in Britain* (London, 1986).

(See also the Nuffield British General Election series, individual volumes of which are cited in the Notes).

BIOGRAPHICAL

J. Adams, *Tony Benn* (London, 1992).

A. Bullock, *The Life and Times of Ernest Bevin*, Vol. 3, *Foreign Secretary 1945–1951* (London, 1983).

T. Burridge, *Clement Attlee. A Political Biography* (London, 1985).

J. Campbell, *Nye Bevan and Mirage of British Socialism* (London, 1987).

S. Crosland, *Tony Crosland* (London, 1982).

B. Donoughue and G. W. Jones, *Herbert Morrison. Portrait of a Politician* (London, 1973).

G. M. F. Drover, *Kinnock. The Path to the Leadership* (London, 1984).

M. Foot, *Aneurin Bevan*, Vol. 2, *1945–60* (London, 1973).

K. Harris, *Attlee* (London, 1982).

R. Harris, *The Making of Neil Kinnock* (London, 1984).

S. Hoggart and D. Leigh, *Michael Foot. A Portrait* (London, 1981).

A. Howard, Crossman. *The Pursuit of Power* (London, 1990).

P. Kellner and C. Hitchens, *Callaghan: The Road to No. 10* (London, 1976).

M. Leapman, *Kinnock* (London, 1987).

D. Marquand, *The Progressive Dilemma. From Lloyd George to Kinnock* (London, 1991).

A. Morgan, *Harold Wilson* (London, 1992).

K. Morgan, *Labour People. Leaders and Lieutenants: Hardie to Kinnock* (Oxford, 1987).

B. Pimlott, *Hugh Dalton* (London, 1985).

P. Williams, *Hugh Gaitskell. A Political Biography* (London, 1979).

DIARIES, MEMOIRS AND CONTEMPORARY WRITING

Joel Barnett, *Inside the Treasury* (London, 1982).

Tony Benn, *Out of the Wilderness: Diaries, 1963–67* (London, 1987).

——, *Office Without Power: Diaries, 1968–72* (London, 1988).

——, *Against the Tide: Diaries, 1973–76* (London, 1989).

——, *Conflicts of Interest: Diaries, 1977–80* (London, 1990).

George Brown, *In My Way* (London, 1971).

James Callaghan, *Time and Chance* (London, 1987).

Barbara Castle, *The Castle Diaries 1964–70* (London, 1974).

——, *The Castle Diaries 1974–76* (London, 1980).

Anthony Crosland, *The Future of Socialism* (London, 1956).

——, *Socialism Now* (London, 1974).

Richard Crossman (ed.), *New Fabian Essays* (London, 1952).

——, *The Diaries of a Cabinet Minister*, 3 vols. (London, 1975–77).

Hugh Dalton, *High Tide and After. Memoirs 1945–60* (London, 1962).

Edmund Dell, *A Hard Pounding. Politics and Economic Crisis 1974–1976* (Oxford, 1991).

Peggy Duff, *Left, Left, Left* (London, 1971).

Michael Foot, *Another Heart and Other Pulses: the Alternative to the Thatcher Society* (London, 1984).

Joe Haines, *The Politics of Power* (London, 1977).

Roy Hattersley, *Choose Freedom: the Future for Democratic Socialism* (London, 1986).

Denis Healey, *The Time of My Life* (London, 1989).

Stuart Holland, *The Socialist Challenge* (London, 1975).

Douglas Jay, *Change and Fortune. A Political Record* (London, 1980).

Roy Jenkins, *A Life at the Centre* (London, 1991).

Ian Mikardo, *Back-Bencher* (London, 1988).

Austin Mitchell, *Four Years in the Death of the Labour Party* (London, 1983).

B. Pimlott (ed.), *The Political Diary of Hugh Dalton 1918–40 and 1945–60* (London, 1986).

Emanuel Shinwell, *Conflict without Malice* (London, 1955).

Marcia Williams, *Inside Number Ten* (London, 1972).

P. Williams (ed.), *The Diary of Hugh Gaitskell 1945–1956* (London, 1983).

Harold Wilson, *The Labour Government 1964–1970. A Personal Record* (London, 1971).

——, *Final Term. The Labour Government 1974–76* (London, 1979).

INDEX

Affluent worker, 36, 56–7
American loan (1945), 14, 20, 31
Ashdown, Paddy,124–5
Asquith, H. H., 2, 4
Attlee, Clement, 1–2, 4, 6–14, 17–18,
 20–1, 25–6, 28–9, 31, 33, 37–45,
 52, 54, 59, 62, 66, 69, 77-8, 98, 105,
 127, 132–3

Barnes, Rosie, 119
Barnett, Joel, 89
Beckett, Margaret, 130
Benn, Tony, 67, 85, 88, 90–2, 96, 104,
 109–11, 115, 117, 122, 135
Berlin Blockade, 21
Bevan, Aneurin, 12, 18–23, 26–9,
 33, 37–8, 40–8, 50, 52, 57, 85,
 135
Bevanites, 27, 35, 37–42, 45–6, 48–9,
 52, 54, 62, 81
Beveridge Report, 7
Beveridge, Sir William, 8
Bevin, Ernest, 4, 9–11, 14–15, 20–2,
 27–8, 32–3, 38, 62
Brown, George, 54, 62–3, 68, 72
By-elections, 42, 48–9, 53, 65, 71, 86,
 96, 112, 115, 118–9, 123–4

Callaghan, James, 2, 54, 60, 62–3, 68–
 9, 72, 75, 83, 87–8, 90, 93–9, 110,
 113, 116, 127, 131–5
Campaign for Democratic Socialism
 (CDS), 52–3
Campaign for Labour Party
 Democracy (CLPD), 98, 111
Campaign for Labour Victory, 108
Campaign for Nuclear Disarmament
 (CND), 48, 51–2, 118
Castle, Barbara, 38, 62, 68, 73–5, 104

Challenge to Britain (1953), 41, 43
Chamberlain, Neville, 6–7
Churchill, Winston, 1, 7, 17–18, 25,
 28–9, 37, 39, 41–2
'Clause Four', 5, 50–1, 57
Coal industry, 16, 19, 84, 86–7, 116
Coalition government (1940–45), 1, 18
Coates, Ken, 82, 104
Cold War, 8–9, 15, 21, 122
Communist party, 67
Comprehensive schools, 46, 61, 65, 77,
 102
Conservative party, 1, 4–7, 13, 16–17,
 19–20, 24–5, 28–9, 33, 36, 41, 43,
 49–50, 55–6, 63, 66, 71, 77, 87, 90,
 96, 100, 106–7, 111, 113–14, 117,
 120, 125–6, 132–3
Cousins, Frank, 52, 62, 67
Cripps, Sir Stafford, 11, 16, 20–3, 25–6,
 28, 44, 76
Crosland, Anthony, 45–6, 68, 79, 85,
 87, 91, 95–6, 105, 115, 122
Crossman, Richard, 37–9, 41, 68–9, 72

Daily Mail, 104
Daily Telegraph, 48
Dalton, Hugh, 11, 14–16, 19–21, 23–5,
 29, 39–40, 42–4
Deakin, Arthur, 38, 40
Delors, Jacques, 123
Devaluation, 23, 63–4, 68–9, 71–3, 79,
 87, 95, 133
Devolution, 100, 104
Donovan, Lord, 73–4
Douglas-Home, Sir Alec, 54–5, 65

Economic policy, 6, 9, 13–17, 19–20,
 22–5, 27, 31, 53–5, 58, 61, 63–5,
 67–9, 72–5, 78–9, 83, 87–9, 91–5,

97–102, 106–7, 111–13, 117, 122–3, 125, 127, 131–3

Eden, Anthony, 42–3, 45, 47

Education Act (1944), 17–18

Education policy, 17–18, 32, 46, 65, 69, 71, 77–8, 97, 119, 125, 131

Equal pay, 61, 70, 77

European Economic Community (EEC), 53–4, 69–70, 78, 85, 90–3, 109, 113, 117, 123, 127

Falklands War, 112

First World War, 1, 4–5, 7, 31

Foot, Michael, 27, 41, 48, 88, 93–4 110–15, 135

Foreign policy, 6, 8–9, 14–15, 21–2, 25–8, 32–3, 37–42, 47–8, 51–4, 64, 69–70, 117, 122, 124

France, 70

Freeman, John, 26

The Future of Socialism (1956), 45–6

Gaitskell, Hugh, 17, 26–7, 33, 38–40, 42, 44–54, 58, 80, 98, 105, 117, 120, 122, 128, 133

General elections, 2
  1918, 1
  1931, 6
  1935, 1
  1945, 1, 7–8, 66
  1950, 24–5
  1951, 28–9, 37
  1955, 42–3
  1959, 49–50
  1964, 55–6, 58
  1966, 65–6
  1970, 76–7
  1974 (Feb.), 86–7
  1974 (Oct.), 89–90
  1979, 1, 82, 100–3
  1983, 106, 112–14, 116, 126–7
  1987, 107, 119–21,
  1992, 107, 124–7

Germany, 1, 7, 15, 32, 40–1, 57, 79

Gordon Walker, Patrick, 64–5

Gould, Bryan, 119, 130

Griffiths, James, 17

Hattersley, Roy, 71, 115, 120–1

Hatton, Derek, 116

Healey, Denis, 69, 72–3, 79, 83, 88–9, 91–7, 104–5, 110–11, 115, 135

Health service charges, 12, 26–7, 54, 69

Heath, Edward, 65–6, 75–6, 83–9, 96

Housing policy, 18, 23, 32, 46, 65, 131

Hudson, Hugh, 131

Immigration, 56, 65, 71

Imperial policy, 8, 22, 45, 64

Independent Labour party (ILP), 4

India, 8, 22

Industry and Society (1957), 48

Inflation, 31, 67, 69, 73, 76, 78, 82–3, 87–8, 91–3, 100, 102, 107, 112, 120

In Place of Fear, (1952) 37–8

In Place of Strife (1969), 74–5, 80, 84, 87, 104

International Monetary Fund (IMF), 83, 95–7

Iraq, 124

Japan, 79, 117

Jenkins, Roy, 68–70, 72–3, 75–7, 85, 88, 90, 104–5, 111

Jay, Douglas, 39–40, 50, 77

Johnson, President Lyndon, 64

Keep Left group, 12, 30, 37

Kenyan Asians, 70

Keynes, Lord, 14

Keynesian economics, 23, 89

Kinnock, Neil, 97–8, 107, 115–25, 127–8, 130

Kissinger, Henry, 91

Korean War, 25, 28, 31

Labour governments:
  1924, 5
  1929–31, 5–6
  1945–51, 8–35, 40, 43, 47, 59–61, 73, 77–8, 81, 131–2
  1964–70, 60–84, 98, 132
  1974–79, 82–3, 88–105, 115, 126, 130

Labour party:
  Annual conference, 12, 35, 39, 41, 47–8, 50–3, 55, 64, 85, 99, 108–10, 116, 118
  Constituency parties, 13, 35, 37, 39, 48, 53, 57, 61, 71, 80, 98, 108–9, 127

National Executive Committee (NEC), 39, 45, 47, 85, 92, 98, 105, 111–12, 116
Parliamentary party (PLP), 11– 12, 37–8, 41, 44, 52, 54, 57, 71, 80, 93, 96, 110–11, 127
Labour's Immediate Programme (1937), 6
Labour's Programme 1973, 85
Liberal Democratic party, 124
Liberal party, 2, 4–6, 27, 29, 53, 56, 83, 86–7, 89–90, 97, 118
Liberal-SDP Alliance, 107, 111–15, 117–21, 127–8
Lib-Lab pact, 97
Lloyd George, David, 1, 4, 27
Local elections, 13, 71, 76, 97, 118–19, 124

MacDonald, Ramsay, 5–7, 12, 100
Macmillan, Harold, 49, 52–3, 66, 107, 120
Major, John, 107, 124–5
Mandelson, Peter, 116, 128
Marquand, David, 105
Marshall Aid, 21, 25, 31
Mikardo, Ian, 30–1, 41, 74
Militant Tendency, 109, 112, 116, 118
Miners' strike, 116–18
Morrison, Herbert, 11–12, 16, 20, 28, 33, 38–40, 42, 44, 116
Mortimer, Jim, 113

National Enterprise Board, 92
National government (1931–39), 1, 5–6
National Health Service (NHS), 8, 18–19, 26, 32, 39, 41, 46, 65, 69, 78, 97, 100, 119, 122, 126, 131
National Insurance Act (1946), 17
Nationalisation, 8, 16–17, 22–3, 27, 39–41, 43, 46, 48–51, 54, 57, 81, 85–6, 92, 96, 103, 109, 115, 117, 122, 132
National Plan, 63, 68, 132
New Fabian Essays (1952), 40
New Statesman, 70–1
North Atlantic Treaty Organisation (NATO), 9, 21–2, 48, 117
Nuclear weapons, 15, 33, 40–1, 47–8, 53, 64, 101, 113, 117–18, 122, 127, 132

Open University, 77
Opinion polls, 21, 28, 43, 48–9, 53, 65, 71, 76, 86–7, 92, 96, 98, 100, 111, 117–18, 120, 122, 124
Owen, David, 109, 111, 115, 118, 120

Palestine, 22
Poll Tax, 123
Poverty, 17, 131
Prentice, Reg, 98
Proportional Representation, 125, 130

Race relations law, 71, 77, 102
Rank and File Mobilising Committee, 109
Reagan, President Ronald, 118
Reselection of MPs, 108
Revisionism, 35–6, 40, 45–6, 50–1, 53–4, 57, 62, 81, 85, 96, 105, 132
Rhodesia, 64
Rodgers, William, 109, 111

Scargill, Arthur, 116
Scottish Nationalist party, 86, 100
Second World War, 1, 6–7, 13, 131
Shinwell, Emanuel, 12, 19–20
Signposts for the Sixties (1961), 53–4
Smith, John, 130
Snowden, Philip, 5, 27
Social Contract, 88–9, 91–2
Social Democratic party, 111, 115, 119, 127
Social security, 8, 17, 97–8
South Africa, 33, 70
Soviet Union, 9, 12, 14–15, 21, 122
Stalin, Joseph, 15, 22, 46
Steel, David, 97, 120
Suez crisis, 32, 45, 47–8

Tatchell, Peter, 112
Taverne, Dick, 86
Taxation, 16, 49, 71, 73, 76, 78, 91, 103, 125, 131
Thatcher, Margaret, 96, 98–100, 102, 104, 106–7, 111–14, 117–18, 120, 122–24, 135
Thompson, E. P., 47
Thorpe, Jeremy, 89, 97
The Times, 117
Tomlinson, George, 17
Trade unions, 3–5, 13, 17, 35–6, 38–40,

48, 51–3, 57, 66–9, 73–5, 80–1,
83–5, 88, 94, 99–100, 102–4, 106,
109, 111, 113, 116–17, 127, 130–1
Tribune, 37, 48
Tribune group, 74, 92, 105

Unemployment, 5–6, 16, 28, 31, 63–4,
69, 73, 76, 78, 83, 87, 89, 91–2, 98,
102–3, 106, 113, 120
United States of America (USA), 5, 9,
14–15, 20–3, 25, 32, 64, 78, 90, 96,
122

Victory for Socialism, 46
Vietnam, 60, 64, 78, 91

Wall Street Crash, 5

Wembley conference, 110–11
Welfare state, 8–9, 24, 28–30, 32, 63,
77–8, 91, 131
Westland affair, 118
What Went Wrong (1979), 82
Wilkinson, Ellen, 12, 17
Williams, Marcia, 62
Williams, Raymond, 47
Williams, Shirley, 109, 111
Wilson, Harold, 2, 12, 22, 26, 39, 41–3,
45, 52, 54–81, 83–90, 92–5, 101,
104–5, 116, 124, 131–4
'Winter crisis' (1947), 19–20
'Winter of discontent' (1979), 83, 99–
101, 103–4, 126
Wood, Deidre, 119

LIVERPOOL
JOHN MOORES UNIVERSITY
TRUEMAN STREET LIBRARY
15-21 WEBSTER STREET
LIVERPOOL L3 2ET
TEL. 051 231 4022/4023